THE ACADEMY III:

Tournament of Champions

By T.Z. Layton

Books for Young Readers

This is a work of fiction. Names, characters, organizations, places, and events are either products of the author's imagination or are used fictitiously.

THE ACADEMY III: TOURNAMENT OF CHAMPIONS
Copyright © 2023, T.Z. Layton
All rights reserved.

No part of this book may be reproduced, or stored in a retrieval system, or transmitted in any form or by any means, electronic, mechanical, photocopying, recording, or otherwise, without express written permission of the publisher.

Published by First Touch Books for Young Readers
Cover design by Robert Ball
Interior by JW Manus

LEWISHAM KNIGHTS

Leo	United States
John	England
Eddy	Bolivia
JoJo	England
Otto	Hungary
Patrick	Ireland
Brock	England
Sami	Lebanon
Caden	England
Logan	England
Riley	England
Aron	Switzerland

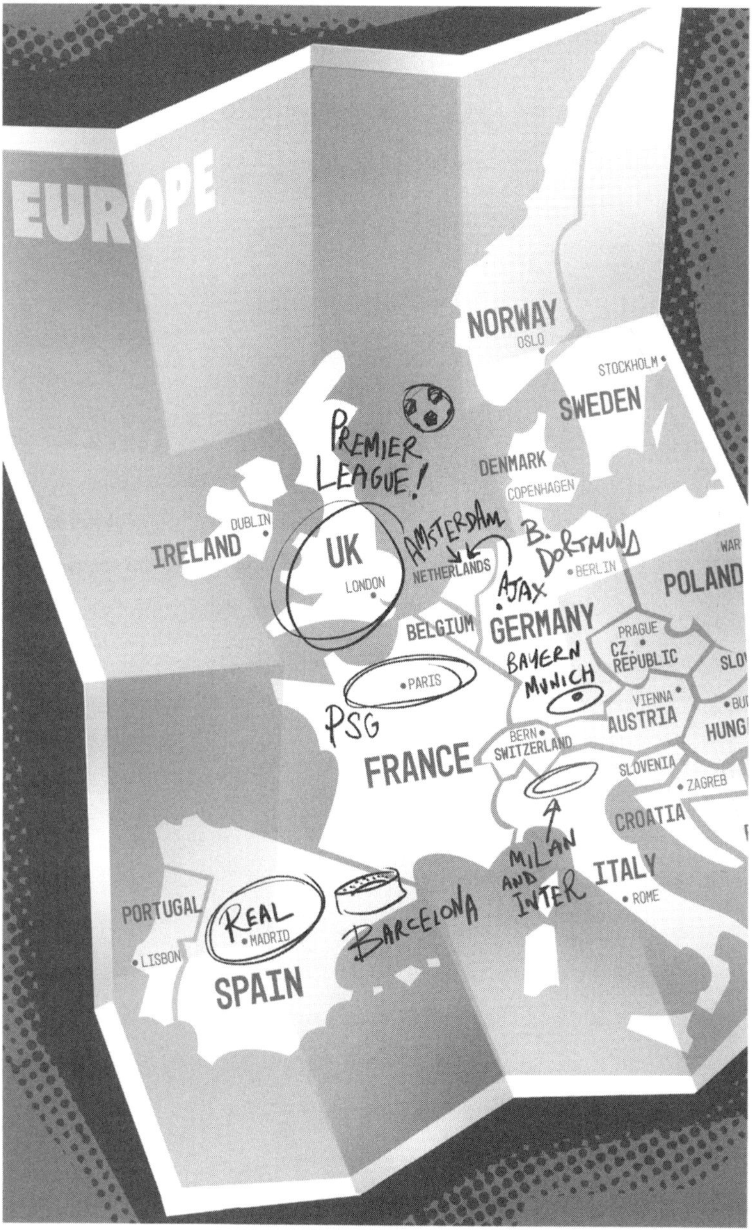
EUROPE
NORWAY
OSLO
STOCKHOLM
SWEDEN
PREMIER LEAGUE!
DENMARK
COPENHAGEN
DUBLIN
IRELAND
UK
LONDON
AMSTERDAM
B. DORTMUND
NETHERLANDS
BERLIN
AJAX
POLAND
BELGIUM
GERMANY
PRAGUE
CZ. REPUBLIC
BAYERN MUNICH
PARIS
VIENNA
AUSTRIA
PSG
BERN
SWITZERLAND
FRANCE
SLOVENIA
ZAGREB
CROATIA
MILAN AND INTER
ITALY
ROME
PORTUGAL
REAL
MADRID
BARCELONA
LISBON
SPAIN

From the Journal of Leo K. Doyle

Note to Readers

Hey there! Would you believe I'm in Paris?

I can hardly believe it myself. I'm not talking about Paris, Ohio either. That's a hiccup of a town not too far from Middleton, where I was born. I'm talking about Paris, France, home to millions of people and the Eiffel Tower and the PSG soccer team.

In fact, I can see the golden lights of the Eiffel Tower right now, as I'm writing in this journal on a night boat ride down a river in the middle of the city. We just played our first game in the Tournament of Champions, which is the best youth competition in all of Europe. It's a lot like the Champions League, which I'm sure you've heard of, but I'll explain all that later. I just wanted to give you a taste of what's going on in my life right now, and what you'll be reading about.

I'm not even going to tell you how our first game went. Not yet. That would spoil the story. But I can tell you we'll also be traveling to Prague and Amsterdam during group play, which is the first stage of the tournament. If we advance, we might go to Berlin or Rome or even Barcelona, where Messi played for most of his career. How amazing would that be?

I'll be honest, though. Advancing past the group stage will be incredibly hard. We're huge underdogs, and lots of people think we shouldn't even be in the tournament. After all, while we saved our team last season, we still finished in second to last place. Most of the teams in the Tournament of Champions finished first or second in their leagues.

And there's more to the story. We have a new coach. Samantha has another commitment this summer, but don't worry, she'll be back for next season. Our new coach is nothing like Coach Purcell—what a relief—but let's just say he . . . does things differently. A *lot* differently. Like, so differently I wonder if he's from the same planet as the rest of us.

We also learned the stakes for the Tournament of Champions are much higher than any of us realized. We won't just be playing for pride and a trophy. I'll tell you about that soon too.

Finally, we have a mystery on our hands. Someone has been trying to sabotage our team. I have no idea who—well, actually, I *do* have a few people in mind. But it's obvious, whoever it is, they want us to lose. I'm worried that if we don't find the guilty person, we won't advance in the tournament no matter how well our team plays.

Whew. That's a lot to deal with, right? You better hang on tight. It's going to be an exciting ride, and we'll get to visit a lot of amazing places. And don't worry—most of all, there will be plenty of soccer. High-stakes, best-in-the-world, edge-of-your-seat soccer.

But first things first. Let's get to the start of this story, where a cocky new kid has just moved to my hometown and thinks he's a better player than the rest of us.

And, you know, maybe he *is* better than we are, me included.

Let's find out, why don't we?

ENTRY #1

Sunshine and Storm Clouds

Two days after beating the London Dragons in the final game of the U14 Premier League season, I flew home to see my family. Two days after that, on the third Saturday in May, I turned thirteen. My dad and Aunt Janice made a big deal about it. They kept telling me over and over that I was officially a teenager. I think they were trying to convince themselves instead of me. From my perspective, it was just another day, though a pretty great one that included all my best friends from back home, a table full of pizza and birthday cake and presents, soccer all day, and video games all night.

Except for the weekends, the rest of May was a little boring, since my friends were still in school. But on June 1, the day they got out for summer, we all raced to the city pool, Breezeland, for the rest of the afternoon.

Breezeland was enormous. On a hot summer day, you could find most of the kids in Middleton swimming in the Olympic-size pool, hanging out at the snack bar, or playing one of the games they have on site: basketball, tennis, Ping-Pong, shuffleboard, and tetherball.

My friends and I liked to play barefoot soccer on the wide grassy lawn where mothers and high school girls spread out their blankets to sunbathe. In fact, after Dennis and I finished trying out new jumps in the diving area and toweled off, we noticed that a game had started. Eager to join in, we headed over and watched for a minute to see which side needed help. The game was eight v eight, with flip-flops for goals. No corner flags, goalies, or out of bounds lines. Just free flowing summer soccer with a ball that had a loose panel flapping like a wounded bird.

All the players were about our age. I recognized Carlos and everyone else except for a tanned kid who looked fourteen or fifteen and was the best player on the field.

Unfortunately, he was shoving that fact down everyone's throat, yelling at his teammates to pass the ball and taunting the opposing players every time he dribbled around someone.

Carlos ran over to us. "About time. Are you two dragon farts ready to join?"

"Who's the new guy?" Dennis asked.

Carlos made a face. "Jackson. He just moved from San Diego and says the soccer out there is way better than here."

"He's pretty good," I said calmly, as I watched him weave through two players and take a shot that just missed. "How old is he?"

"He'll be in high school next year. My brother said the coach already promised him a starting position."

"Let's go!" Jackson yelled as the other players stopped to wait for me and Dennis to join. "Are you two coming in or not?" He waved a hand at the other team. "You can have the big kid because we're winning."

Dennis—the "big kid"—grinned and slapped me on the back. "Hey Leo, it's been a while since you weren't the first choice, huh?"

"Not really. I wasn't even a starter until halfway through the season. But listen, why don't you play with the new guy? Maybe I can even things up a bit."

"If you're playing," Dennis said, "the teams aren't going to be even no matter what."

"Don't worry, I'll take it easy."

"Please don't," Carlos said, as Jackson crossed his arms with impatience. "I'm already tired of this guy's mouth, and we just met."

After Dennis stripped off his shirt to play with the skins, Jackson frowned and held up his palms. "Didn't I say to join the other team? I need some competition."

Dennis snorted. "I'm not that good. And trust me, there wouldn't be enough competition if everyone *but* Leo joined our team."

"What are you talking about? Who's Leo?"

As the game restarted, Dennis jogged to the middle of the field, shaking his head and chuckling. I hung back on defense until someone passed the ball to Jackson. He raced down the sideline, heading straight for Carlos, who was two years younger and weighed about ninety pounds when he was soaking wet and carrying a sack of potatoes. It's true that size doesn't matter that much in soccer, and my best friend was pretty good, but he didn't have enough skill to make up the age gap. Carlos tried a slide tackle that fell just short, and Jackson skipped away, angling inside.

"Pass!" one of his teammates yelled. "Cross it!"

But Jackson only had eyes for the goal. I was the last line of defense, and he dribbled straight towards me, determined to score. Time slowed to a crawl in the boiling Ohio sun as the other players stopped running to watch the one v one battle.

There wasn't much to it. Jackson was much bigger than me and indeed a very good player. But he wasn't ready for the Premier League. Not even close. As he darted in, trying for a feint to the left that his body language gave away, I stuck out a leg, poked the ball behind him, and collected it on the other side. Then I looked up and spied our center forward, Nate, snow-birding by our opponent's goal. I chipped a pass all the way across the field that landed right at Nate's feet. He missed the trap, and the ball skirted to the side, but no one else was close, so he recovered and scored.

"That was lucky," Jackson grumbled as he passed me on his way back for the kickoff.

Soon after, Carlos stole the ball in midfield and passed to me. I made a point to veer towards Jackson, who ran straight at me, determined to get some payback. As he snarled and dove in for the tackle, I did a lightning quick one-two dribble and slid past him like an eel slipping through water. I heard him grunt in surprise as I made another pinpoint pass to Nate, who was alone again up front.

Nate poked it between the two flip-flops for another goal, and I turned to Jackson. "I guess I was lucky again."

Jackson's face screwed up as if he couldn't quite comprehend what had just happened. "I didn't know you were any good," he said. "Who do you play for? The Tigers? That's the best club team around."

"The Knights."

"The Knights? What team is that?"

"The *Lewisham* Knights," Carlos said as he walked over. "You know, the Premier League? And he went to the London Dragons Academy before that."

Jackson started laughing. "I get it, you're roasting the new guy. No, really. Where do you play?"

"In London," I said. "I'm here for a short break, then I'm flying back. We're competing in a summer tournament in Europe."

"It's like the Champions League," Carlos added. "For U14s."

Jackson couldn't seem to stop blinking. "Ch-ch-champions League? *Premier* League? You mean you really play for the *Lewisham Knights*?"

"Their youth team," I corrected, as Jackson's tanned jaw seemed to fall all the way to the grass.

"So," Carlos said with a smirk, "what do you think about soccer around here now?"

We played for another hour. I took it easy and only used my left foot so I wouldn't dominate the game too much. I just wanted to have fun with my friends. It turns out Jackson was an okay guy once his ego was taken down a few notches.

After we finished the game and downed some ice-cold Gatorade, we played tetherball and then beach volleyball, where I guess Californians really do have an advantage, because Jackson was much better than the rest of us.

Cooling off in the pool.

Hot dogs and burgers and ice cream at the snack bar.

More tetherball and volleyball and a final round of cannonballs off the diving boards.

We stayed at Breezeland until they closed the gates at dusk. Carlos and Dennis and I walked home together as the crickets and cicadas sang in the trees. The warm night air felt good after nine months in dreary England. Life in general felt good, and I was looking forward to a summer in Europe seeing cities I'd only dreamed about and testing myself against some of the best youth players in the world.

Dennis started cracking up as we entered our neighborhood. "Did you see the look on Jackson's face when he heard Leo played for a Premier League team? I wish someone had recorded that."

"Don't worry," Carlos said. "I won't let anyone forget it. So, Leo, when do you leave?"

"Sunday."

"I only have two more days to roast you? Are you nervous?"

"About what?"

"About what? Oh, let's see. Playing FIFA against us tonight? Playing hide and go seek with your sister in the backyard? Are you nervous about *playing in the Tournament of Champions*?"

Carlos always made me laugh. "Oh. That. Not really."

"I don't believe you."

"Alright. I'm a little nervous. Maybe a lot. But there was so much pressure last season that a summer tournament feels like a vacation. Plus, we're going to be giant underdogs. We'll do our best to win, but it's not like our season is riding on the outcome."

"What if Messi comes to watch you play?"

"I don't think that's going to happen."

"But it could. Or any number of star players. Am I right?"

"Well . . . I guess."

"You see?" Carlos said with satisfaction.

"Are you *trying* to make me nervous?"

"No. I just like being right. Which I always am."

I rolled my eyes as Dennis swatted Carlos on the shoulder.

"We need regular updates," Carlos said. "At every city you visit."

"Got it," I said solemnly.

"And much more swag. A jersey from every team."

"Uh, yeah. I'll do my best."

"Signed by the top players."

"If I meet any, I'll tell them you asked."

"You better."

On Saturday evening, the night before I left for England, Dad called me to dinner with Ginny and Aunt Janice. As usual, I had requested spaghetti and meatballs and garlic bread, made with my mom's recipe.

When I arrived at the table, Dad shot me an irritated look. "Leo, put a shirt on."

"It's hot in here."

"The AC guy's coming on Monday. I'm sorry it's hot, but we wear shirts at the dinner table. You know the rules."

I left the room and returned wearing a black-and-silver Knights practice jersey. Soon Ginny came in wearing headphones and dancing. When she sat down, Dad asked her to remove the headphones.

"What?" Ginny said, far too loudly.

"I said, *take the headphones off at dinner!*"

Indignant, Ginny removed the headphones and tossed them on a chair behind her. "Geez. You don't need to shout."

"Apparently I do. And don't throw your headphones, young lady. Do you know how expensive those were?"

"All right, everyone," Aunt Janice said as she walked in carrying a loaf of garlic bread fresh from the oven. "Let's all relax. It's our last night with Leo for a while."

Dad pursed his lips and looked off to the side. "I'm just a little . . ." He turned towards me and forced a smile. "I'm gonna miss you, kiddo. Again."

"We all will," Aunt Janice said. "But at least we'll have a lot more food around. Do you want three meatballs or four, Leo?"

"Ten."

She sighed and dished me a huge portion. During dinner, Dad lectured me on how to stay safe in strange cities, Aunt Janice made me promise to absorb the local culture every place I went, and Ginny stole the last piece of garlic bread and took a bite before I could protest.

I spent the rest of the evening packing for the trip and talking to Messi, my pet bearded dragon. I was going to miss him terribly and felt guilty about leaving again, so I fed him lots of juicy crickets and let him strut around the room like an emperor.

My flight from Columbus didn't leave until six in the evening, so I slept until nine and had banana pancakes for breakfast. When I returned to my room and picked up my device, I realized I had a new text on WhatsApp. The text was from Brock, which surprised me. We had exchanged numbers but had never talked online.

Did you see the news, Yank?

> About what?

The Knights. I mean the EPL Knights. They got relegated.

Relegated means *sent down*, and *EPL* is short for *English Premier League*. With all the chaos surrounding my trip and leaving home again, I had forgotten that today was the final day of the adult Premier League season. I knew the Lewisham Knights weren't doing so well and were in danger of relegation to the Championship League, which is the second tier of English professional soccer.

I pulled up a web browser, checked the news, and saw that Brock was right: In a devastating end to the season, the Knights had lost 2–1 to the team just below them in the Premier League Table. All of a sudden, I realized what that might mean, and a pit opened in my stomach as my fingers whirled across the keyboard.

> Wait. Are we getting relegated too?

Yeah, genius. We are. Not all youth teams follow their EPL parent teams up or down, but we do. My dad checked with the coaches.

This was terrible news. After a season in the Youth Premier League, playing in the second division would be a giant step backward. It would be especially cruel after finishing the season so well. I felt like our team had finally come together and that we might even have a chance to challenge the Dragons for the title next season.

But not if we weren't playing in the top division.

That wasn't the only thing. Playing in the second division could hurt our future careers. I supposed I could look for another team, one that would be playing in the top division next season, but there was no guarantee I would find one. And I didn't *want* another team.

I wanted to play for the Knights. With my friends.

I put my head in my hands and paced back and forth. Messi was standing on his hind legs and glaring at me with his beady eyes for some reason.

When I sat down again, there was another message from Brock.

> **U still there?**

> Yeah.

> **Before you start feeling too sorry for yourself, listen up. We have one chance to avoid getting sent down.**

I sat up straight.

> We do? What?

> **My dad and I did some research. You know how in the Europa League the winner qualifies for the Champions League next season? And the Champions League winner gets an automatic place too?**

I didn't know all of that and was surprised that Brock had spent his Sunday doing research. Then again, Brock was extremely competitive, and lived and breathed Premier League soccer.

I texted:

> Okay. How does that help us?

Our league has something like that too. There's an old loophole that says the winners of the Tournament of Champions get automatic spots in their division of the Youth Premier League the next season. I don't think many people know about the loophole because the teams that play in the Tournament of Champions are never in danger of relegation.

> Except us.

Right. Except us. Anyway, this thing is real, Yank. We can stay in the Youth Premier League next season. All we have to do is win this tournament.

ENTRY #2

Fair is a Word That Applies to the Weather

After the talk with Brock, I went outside and began juggling a soccer ball, lost in my thoughts. Life had finally seemed calm again. I was leaving on an exciting trip to Europe with my friends and teammates, and when we got back, we'd be playing in the Youth Premier League next season.

Now everything had changed. My future felt out of control, sprawling in every direction, like an octopus flopping around on the shore, trying to get back to water.

I returned inside and found Messi staring at me from the highest branch of his fake tree, his little beard flared in anger. At first I was annoyed. *Give me a break already! I just got some really bad news.*

But I knew what he was trying to say. Messi had a sixth sense about my life and its problems.

The news from Brock wasn't the end of the world.

It was just a challenge that needed to be met.

I took a deep breath. Whether or not we played in the Youth Premier League next season was up to us. Brock and I and the rest of our teammates. We just had to accomplish one eensy-weensy tiny little thing.

Take first place in a tournament with the best teams our age in all of Europe.

On the way to the Columbus airport in my dad's truck, with Aunt Janice snoring in the back seat and Ginny tuning out the world on her headphones, I told my dad the bad news about the team.

"Relegation?" he said. "I don't understand what that is."

I thought about how to explain it. "Think about it like this. What happens when a team comes in last place in the NBA or the NFL or the MLB?"

"Well," Dad said, "the fans aren't happy. And the worst teams get better odds in the draft the next year."

"But do they get *punished*?"

"Not really, except for the money they lose from poor attendance. I guess they even get rewarded because of the draft."

"Exactly. But it's not that way in England. In the Premier League, every single year, the worst three teams drop down to the lower division. And the top three teams in the second division move up to the Premier League."

My dad's eyebrows lifted. "Really? That's relegation? They get moved to the . . . minor leagues?"

"Yep. It's still the pros, but that's probably the best way to think about it."

"But that's . . . unbelievable. I can't even imagine that happening over here. The fans and players would hate it."

"They're not too happy about it in England either. Sometimes the players get their salaries cut in half."

"I see what you mean," he said slowly. "Relegation is a big deal. Huh. It's kind of an interesting model, though, isn't it?

Teams would never lose on purpose or tank their season. And it makes the season meaningful even for the losing teams. Whew. So that's what will happen if you don't win this tournament? Even though it wasn't your fault?"

"That's right."

My dad's strong jaw worked back and forth. "That doesn't seem fair. But as my own pop used to say, fair is a word that applies to the weather."

"Dad. You know I hate it when you say that."

"Listen, Leo. You're young and you'll have plenty of chances to prove yourself, even if your team is relegated to the lower division. It doesn't help to sit around and worry. That will only make you miserable. Don't sweat it, okay?"

"I'll try," I mumbled.

"After that, well, I suppose your team better go to this tournament prepared to play."

I stared out the window at the cars rushing past on the Interstate. "Yeah. That's what Messi said."

At the airport, my family threw another embarrassing hugging party in front of all those strangers. Then, just like the last two times, my dad took me through security and waited at the gate until it was time to board.

I was alone on the plane this time. No Tig or Samantha to keep me company. I didn't mind. Flying was easy now. I kicked back, watched a movie, read a manga, ate some snacks, and gazed out of the window. On my first solo flight, for some reason I couldn't explain, I felt as if my mom was with me. So I didn't feel lonely at all.

When I landed at Heathrow Airport in London, a team manager met me at the gate and drove me to the Caravan, the home of the Knights Youth Academy. I was disappointed we didn't take the subway, and the traffic to Lewisham was awful. Rain was pouring down, I was jetlagged from the flight, and the news about the relegation still weighed heavily on my mind.

But all of that melted away when I walked through the tall iron gate and saw the silver sign with black letters announcing the entrance to the Lewisham Knights Player Development Academy. A tingle of pride ran through me, and I remembered I was about to see my friends and teammates. I even stopped worrying about the tournament, because if anyone could figure out a way to carry us to victory, it was Samantha.

Thunder rumbled overhead. Huddled under an umbrella, I walked alongside the line of practice fields with smooth green grass and giant light poles, awed all over again by how far I had come from the muddy, uneven YMCA fields in my hometown. As I entered the aging brick building where the U14s lived—my building—even the musty smell and worn rugs felt cozy and familiar.

Coach Luca, our player development manager, stepped out of his office near the entrance. "*Ciao*, Leo! Welcome back! You're the last to arrive."

"I am?"

"Why don't you drop your bags in your room and go to the lounge? Everyone's there. Samantha will be in soon and has some announcements to make during lunch."

"About what?"

He patted me on the back, took my umbrella, and set it by the door. "You'll just have to see."

Curious, I dropped my bags in my third-floor room (the second floor in England) and hurried downstairs. Right after I stepped through the lounge door, I saw a blur on my left, one with a crewcut and a smashed bulldog face. Brock roared "Yank!" as his burly arms picked me up from behind and lifted me in the air.

I heard John's London accent next. "Leo, bruv!"

They were all there: Otto with his huge forehead and owlish eyes, Eddy dancing in place to celebrate my arrival, Patrick uttering a string of nonsense words and doing a split right there on the floor, Sami greeting me with his quiet and shy manner, JoJo tipping her head in my direction and sneering a little less than usual, Riley muttering under his breath so low that I only caught "Leo" and "madferit," whatever that meant.

Even Caden and Logan came over to fist bump me, which I took as a sign of peace. I had figured they would hate my guts forever, so it was a relief to know I wouldn't be fighting with them all summer.

I realized two people were missing. "Where's Taye and Ajay?"

Eddy stopped dancing and flopped his big body on a sofa. His dark hair was cut shorter than usual. "Taye's leg needs another month to heal. He'll be back for the season. So will Ajay, but his parents are making him study all summer."

I blinked a few times. "Why?"

"Prep for entrance exams," John said. I noticed his stubby dreadlocks had grown another inch, and he was still as short and solid as a fire hydrant. "They want to put him in a top school if football doesn't work out."

"Don't they realize this is the *Tournament of Champions*?"

"Yeah, Ajay's not too chuffed."

"Can't he study at night or something?"

"I don't know, bruv."

"That's awful."

"Actually," Otto said, "it's quite intelligent. Even at the academies, only a tiny percentage of players become professionals. The rest will have to get another job. Ajay's parents are looking out for his future in case a professional football career doesn't work out."

The rest of us stared at Otto in disbelief. Brock threw a pillow at him.

"Hi, everyone," said a bright, cheerful, familiar voice.

We all turned and saw Samantha standing in the doorway with a wide smile and a duffel bag slung over her shoulder. She was wearing jeans and Adidas flats and a long-sleeve Knights shirt. Her brown hair was caught in a ponytail and damp from the rain.

"Coach Sam!" John called out as we all ran over to mob her.

"All right," she laughed, throwing out high-fives and fist bumps. "I hope everyone had a great break, though I know it was short. Why don't we head to the cafeteria? I've got a few announcements to make, including your first opponent in the Tournament of Champions."

"Wait," Brock said. "You know who we're playing?"

"I know the whole group. Come on, let's talk over lunch. I'm starving."

I was hungry, too, as well as eager to hear these mysterious announcements. Once Coach Luca came down, we followed him and Samantha to the cafeteria, piled our trays with food, and made our way to our seats. I sat between John and Eddy, with Otto and Sami right across from me.

Samantha stood at the podium, took a drink of water, and unwrapped a sandwich. "I've got some good news and some, well, other news." Her expression darkened. "First off, let's get something out of the way. I'm sure by now you've all heard the news about our relegation."

This caused a collective groan.

"I didn't sign up for the second-best league," Caden muttered.

"We don't deserve this," Brock added. "Not after last season."

"I agree," Samantha said evenly. "Unfortunately, we often don't get what we deserve in life."

She didn't deserve to get injured and have her pro career ruined, I thought, knowing she would never say that out loud.

"All we can do is move forward," she continued. "Deal with reality. And our reality, team, is that there *is* a way back into the Youth Premier League—by winning the Tournament of Champions. I'm sure you all know this, since multiple parents have contacted me."

We all nodded.

"Good," she said. "So we know where we stand and what we have to do. Next, a little good news. The Dragons aren't playing in the tournament. They've decided to tour the US and Mexico instead."

I whistled. That *was* good news. Our fiercest rival, a team that most people still thought was the best team our age in England, wouldn't even be playing.

"The Dragons are only the third-best team in the U14

UEFA rankings," Otto declared. "And the top two are in the tournament. Paris Saint-Martin and Real Madrid."

"Thank you, Otto," Samantha said drily. "As always, your scholarship is impressive."

"All the other teams are in the top twenty-five."

"Yes. Duly noted. Winning the tournament will be a very, very difficult task."

"But we'll do it, right?" Brock said. "You've got a plan?"

"Of course you can do it. I believe in each and every one of you." She took a deep breath, and I could sense more bad news coming. "But I'm sorry to say I won't be your coach for the summer."

ENTRY #3

A Lesson in Pasta

"Wait, wut?" Riley said, his crooked front teeth sticking out as his face scrunched in confusion.

John stood up. "Noooooo. Coach Sam, what gives?"

Everyone else was speechless. As John sank back down, I felt as if someone had just pulled my chair out from under me.

The news about our relegation hadn't seemed quite so awful with Samantha in charge. I trusted her to find a way for us to win the Tournament of Champions. Also, she had just been appointed our coach, and none of us had forgotten, not for a second, what life was like under Coach Purcell. We all loved Samantha and couldn't bear the thought of her leaving.

"I don't understand," I said. "Did you take a new job?"

She smiled. "Do you think I'd abandon you after a season like that? I can't *wait* to coach you in the fall. But here's the thing. Since this is my first head coaching job, I have to get licensed. I was on my way last season but not quite there. There's a test I have to take over the summer."

"What do you mean?" Brock said. "You coached us for half a season!"

"True, but I was an interim coach. There are different rules in place for a mid-season change. To make it official, I have to get properly licensed."

"Can't you do that online or something?" I said. "While the tournament is going on?"

She shook her head. "I wish. All the licensing tests and clinics are scheduled over the summer so coaches and managers don't miss time during the season. I have to be here in person. I'm sorry, but that's just the way it is."

Though I was relieved she wasn't leaving us, who would lead our team over the summer?

"Coach Luca?" Eddy asked. "Will you be in charge?"

Samantha answered for him. "He'll be my assistant next year but is going through the same process I am." As we began to murmur in confusion, she held up a hand for quiet. "Although I won't be coaching you, Mr. Haddad and the Board understand the situation and have put the highest priority on winning the Tournament of Champions. They've hired one of the top coaches in the *world* to guide you over the summer."

This caused a flurry of excitement. One of the top coaches in the world? Who could that be? And how could they coach a different team over the summer?

She said, "Do you know who Giuseppe Grifone is?"

Brock threw his palms on the table. "*What*? Beppe Grifone is going to coach *us*? A youth team?"

It took me a second, but then I recognized the name. Beppe Grifone was a Spanish manager who had coached in all the best leagues, including the Premier League and La Liga, the top division in Spain. Beppe had even managed the Spanish national team.

"But he announced his retirement over the summer," Otto said. "After leaving Atletico Madrid."

"That's true," Samantha said. "Which is why he's free to coach. Mr. Haddad knows him personally, explained the situation, and Beppe thought it would be fun to work with a youth team. Also, Beppe started his playing career in Lewisham many years ago, so he has ties to the club. It still took a lot to convince him—"

"You mean a lot of money," Brock barked.

Samantha spread her hands. "However he got here, this is an incredible opportunity. Beppe Grifone is prolonging his retirement for another month to guide *you* through the Tournament of Champions."

I was stunned by this announcement. We get to play for a real professional coach? This *was* good news. None of us clapped or said much, since we all would miss Samantha and didn't want to hurt her feelings, but I felt a little better about the summer.

"Something else," Samantha said. "We have a new recruit. He won't arrive until tonight, but he'll be at practice tomorrow."

This caused us all to glance around nervously, wondering what position the new recruit played and whether it would impact our own playing time. I know that wasn't the best reaction, and I was prepared to fight for my position, but I couldn't help worrying.

"He plays on the right wing," Samantha continued, "and he's from Switzerland."

That allowed me to relax. Ajay was our right winger, and he wouldn't even be here for the summer.

"Surely you don't mean Aron Eggenburger?" Otto said.

Samantha chuckled. "You do keep up with the news, don't you? That's him. Aron is now a U14 Lewisham Knight."

I turned to Otto. "You know this guy? Who is he?"

"Only the best winger in Switzerland, maybe all of Central Europe. He played for FC Basel last season and was the top scorer in the Swiss league." He turned back to Samantha. "That's an impressive acquisition."

"Thank you, Otto," she said solemnly. "We've had our eye on Aron all season and decided to fast-track him to help with the tournament."

Okay, I thought. *Even if Ajay was here, he's still learning how to play on the wing. A top scorer like Aron can definitely help us.*

"So what about the tournament?" Brock said. "Who do we play first?"

Samantha finished chewing a bite of sandwich. "The Tournament of Champions has thirty-two teams, divided into eight groups with four teams each. Just like the World Cup. In the first round, the teams in each group will play each other once, for a total of three games per team. After that, the top two teams in each group will advance to the knockout rounds." She paused for a drink of water. "We're in Group D along with Prague FC, Paris Saint-Martin, and Perseus Amsterdam."

I raised a hand. "Where are the games?"

"In the Tournament of Champions," she continued, "the higher-ranked team always plays at home. At least until the championship game, which is in Paris this year. Unfortunately, because we're the lowest ranked team in the whole tournament, all of our games will be away games. On the other hand, you'll get to see a lot of new cities. Our first game is six days from now, on Sunday evening, against Paris Saint-Martin."

Paris sounded like an exciting destination, and a cheer broke out. But I wasn't familiar with that particular team. "Are they part of PSG?"

"Nope. They're based in a different part of Paris."

That made sense. Like London, which has a number of Premier League clubs—Chelsea, Arsenal, and Tottenham, to name a few—Paris was a huge city and would have multiple teams.

"They're even better than PSG," Otto said. "At least the U14s are. Paris Saint-Martin is the number one ranked team our age in all of Europe."

"That's right," Samantha said gravely. "This will be a tough hill to climb, Knights."

After lunch, I spent the rest of the rainy day hanging out in the lounge and the rec room, catching up with my friends and practicing some tricks on the indoor field. By the time dinner rolled around, I was feeling loopy from jetlag. But I had learned from past mistakes, when I had fallen asleep too early and woken up in the middle of the night on the first day of practice. This time, I pushed through until 9 p.m., then collapsed on my bed and fell into a deep and dreamless sleep.

The last thing I remembered was being excited for practice the next day—and ready to see if the new recruit could play.

The next morning, Tuesday, began with a layer of mist so thick I could barely see out of the window. Not that unusual for London. With a yawn, I hopped out of bed feeling refreshed and ready to go.

At breakfast, Coach Luca announced that Coach Beppe had just stopped by his office and requested the players report to practice barefoot and to carry their cleats and socks in their kit bags.

What? Barefoot?

Everyone else seemed as startled as I was. Even Samantha, who would be with us at practice this week. Huh. Maybe the new coach wanted to give us all a pair of new cleats.

But couldn't he do that after practice?

Sami raised a hand. "Um, did Coach Beppe say why?"

Coach Luca lifted his palms as if apologizing. "I wish I could tell you."

On my way out of the cafeteria, I asked Samantha if she or Coach Beppe was leading practice.

"Coach Beppe," she said firmly. "He has decades of experience at the highest level. I'm hoping to learn from him just like you."

With a shrug, I took off my socks and shoes and headed outside with the rest of the team, feeling funny as I walked barefoot down the brick path to the field. The other youth teams were still on break, so we had the academy to ourselves. The grass was cold and wet with dew, and the air so filled with mist that it felt like walking through a dream.

When we arrived at the main practice field, I saw two new faces emerge from the fog: a short man with a fringe of white hair, bushy eyebrows that sprung out in all directions, and a belly as round as a soccer ball. This must be Coach Beppe, though he was not carrying a clipboard or a whistle and was dressed in strange attire for a soccer coach: loose-fitting brown trousers and a long-sleeved white shirt with a V-neck and wide sleeves. The outfit resembled something that a monk or a martial arts teacher might wear, instead of a soccer coach.

Just like us, he was barefoot.

Beside him, juggling a soccer ball with great skill, was a dark-haired player our age but who stood half a foot taller than the older man. The player was even taller than Brock and Eddy, and almost as tall as Diego or Tig. The new guy wasn't skinny either. He had thick leg muscles, a broad chest, and defined arms that made me self-conscious about my own skinny frame. He wasn't quite as heavy as Brock or Otto, but he looked more athletic than both of them, and his short hair was styled even more perfectly than Caden's, sticking up high in a flat top that made him appear even taller.

"Team," Samantha said as she walked towards the two of them, "meet Aron, your new teammate, and Coach Beppe."

One by one, she introduced every player to the newcomers. Aron stopped juggling but seemed bored by the introductions, while Coach Beppe beamed a grandfatherly smile every time Samantha called out a new name and told him where we were from and our position.

"The United States?" he asked when I was announced. "Good, good. Where is this Ohio? Close to New York or California?"

"Not really," I said. "It's in the middle of the country, near the Great Lakes. The Midwest."

"Ah," he said with a knowing look. "Chicago."

"Kind of. The closest cities are Columbus and Cincinnati."

"Ah. *Sí.*" It was clear he had no idea what I was talking about. "*Bueno*, Leo, it's very nice to make your acquaintance."

The new coach might not know my country very well, but at least he seemed nice.

"Now," Coach Beppe said, bringing his hands together with

a sharp clap. "I'm pleased to see that everyone has respected my request and arrived barefoot. You will see that I do things a little differently from other coaches. I will ask you now to please sit on the ground, cross-legged, and place your hands on your legs. Like this."

All at once, he lowered to the ground, much faster and smoother than I would have thought someone his size and age could move. I could tell he used to be an excellent athlete, and remembered he had a legendary playing career before he became a coach.

We all followed his lead, sitting on the damp ground with our legs crossed and our arms resting on our thighs. Coach Beppe began to take deep slow breaths and asked us to do the same. The mist was so thick it seemed to settle on my hands and face as I breathed in and out, shivering from the cool air.

"Excellent," he said. "It is good to clear the head before you play, and to become one with the earth. Never forget that true football is a game that takes place in nature, on the grass beneath our feet. To maximize your potential, you must connect with the planet. Who is most at home in Mother Nature, I ask you? The animals of field and stream and jungle. You should strive to be like them. At one with your environment. Feeling the grass and the soil and the pulse of the atoms beneath you. Wiggle your toes, now. Scrunch your feet into the grass as you breathe. Good, good, good."

Okay, I thought, *this guy is definitely nothing like Coach Purcell.*

Or anyone else I've ever met.

I caught Aron rolling his eyes, and someone behind me snickered. Caden or Logan, I guessed.

"Laughter is okay," Coach Beppe said. "It is a learning process. I had a lesson planned with the bumblebees but unfortunately, they are not out this morning. They cannot navigate without the sun, you see. Now!" He clapped again and jumped to his feet. "Let's replace our socks and boots and warm up. You have a procedure in place for this, I assume?"

"Yes," Samantha said, with a little smile on her lips.

"Good. I will not adjust it. Let me know when you are finished."

After we all put on our socks and cleats, Samantha led us through a familiar warmup: three slow laps around the field, five Carolinas for conditioning, and a round of stretching. While this was happening, I noticed Coach Beppe staring at a tree on the sideline with a thoughtful expression. I assumed he was thinking about the genius soccer tactics he was about to teach us.

When warmups were finished, Coach Beppe put on his shoes and gathered everyone in a huddle. Next to him was a line of cones that stretched across the width of the field in an unusual pattern that resembled a tight spiral or a corkscrew. The sky had begun to spit rain, and I wished I'd brought a long-sleeve shirt. Was this June or November?

"*Bueno*," he said, clasping his hands atop his bulging stomach. "Shall we proceed to our first drill?"

Finally, I thought, eager to learn at the feet of this great teacher.

He reached into a pocket and took out something which he concealed in his left fist. "Since we are new to each other, there is something you should know about me. More than anything other than football, I love to eat, as I am sure you can tell." He grinned as he patted his belly with his other hand.

"And I especially love pasta. I am not Italian but have often thought I should have been born in Rome, so much do I love these little concoctions of water and flour."

He held out his left hand and opened it, revealing a piece of dried pasta with a similar shape to the cones on the field. "Behold the fusilli. I've found the shape of pasta to be quite instructive for football. Simple, timeless patterns with complex and profound meanings. Today the fusilli will instruct us, and I will interpret its teachings. Okay? Good? *Sí*? Ball, please."

Coach Luca passed him a ball, which Coach Beppe trapped and dribbled to the first cone.

"Observe," he said, then took off with the ball towards the next cone. When he reached it, he spun around it, quick as a rattlesnake's strike, and darted to another. He proceeded to weave in and out of all the cones, sometimes whirling around them, sometimes feinting one way and moving the other. When he returned to the huddle, a little out of breath, he said, "You understand? You can do this?"

I exchanged a look with John, who was right next to me.

Patrick was on my other side. He whispered, "And I thought I was playing with a different deck."

"Um, Coach," Sami said. "We might need to see that again."

Coach Beppe seemed disappointed. "Okay. Watch again. No, even better—follow behind me."

We each grabbed a ball and did as he asked. I was the last in line. As I dribbled through the cones, I realized that by the time Coach Beppe's pattern made its way back to me, it had gotten lost along the way. I asked him to run through it again and moved closer to the front. On about the tenth try, everyone finally got it right, and we were able to weave faster through the fusilli cones.

"The cones are defenders," he called out as he watched us. "Don't give them access to the ball. Always be ready to protect what is yours."

For the next drill, he replaced the cones with players, and asked them to act as defenders and try to steal the ball. Although the defenders weren't supposed to move—they could only stick out a leg—it added quite a bit of difficulty as we maneuvered through the cones.

When that was finished, we formed two lines and ran a passing drill, weaving through the fusilli pattern using wall passes, give and go's, and overlaps.

We did this all the way until lunch time.

⚽ ⚽ ⚽

When we returned from the cafeteria, some of the fog had lifted, but we found Coach Beppe waiting by the cones, ready to continue with more drills. I couldn't help raising my hand.

"Yes?" he said.

"I was just curious, Coach Beppe, if we're going to scrimmage?"

I cringed after I asked the question, thinking about how Coach Purcell would have responded. He would have pointed at the sideline and barked an order to start running.

"Scrimmage?" he said. "Is that what everyone would like to do?"

Everyone clapped and agreed.

"Ah." He beamed. "Excellent idea. Do we have any pennies?"

"Plenty," Samantha said.

One of the team managers removed the cones from the field, and another handed out the practice pennies: black for the starters, and silver for the second team. "Let's give Aron a silver penny," Samantha said, then threw a quick glance at Coach Beppe. "If that's okay?"

"Of course, of course."

Before we took our positions, Coach Beppe gathered everyone around him. "During the scrimmage," he said, eying each of us in turn, "there is one very important thing I wish for you to do." We waited expectantly, ready for a golden nugget of soccer wisdom that would transform us instantly into better players or hold the key to winning the Tournament of Champions.

"As you play," our coach said in a satisfied voice, "I would like you to remember the fusilli."

ENTRY #4

An Unexpected Challenge

The gray sky began to spit rain as Samantha blew the whistle for the scrimmage to begin. I bounced on my toes, happy to be playing again, feeling as if our team break had lasted a few months instead of a few weeks. Time off from soccer? Who needs that?

I was also ready to impress Coach Beppe. Despite his . . . interesting . . . coaching methods, he was a professional with tons of experience.

The second team kicked off and passed the ball around their half of the field. Logan was their center mid. He received the ball, started to pass back to the defense, then whipped around and tried a long chip to Aron on the right wing.

I knew why Samantha had put Aron on the second team. No matter how good he had been in the Swiss league, this was a new team, and she wanted him to earn his position. I respected that. To Aron's credit, he didn't complain. In fact, when she told him, he had given her a small, confident smile.

Logan's pass soared over Aron's head and skidded down the line, heading towards the corner flag. The closest defender was Eddy, our dancing left fullback from Bolivia. He sprinted back as Brock slid over from the middle to help cover.

Aron reached the ball first, running it down a few steps before it went out of bounds. Whoa, he was fast! With a flick of his foot, he rolled the ball backwards, turned, and saw Brock and Eddy closing in. Normally Brock would back off and let Eddy be the first line of defense, but the way Brock was charging forward with his head down made me think he wanted to prove a point to the new guy.

Aron was trapped in the corner with no place to go. Eddy and Brock, two of our biggest players, were about to arrive at the same time and make a pancake out of our new recruit. After scanning the field for his options, Aron lifted the ball in the air with his instep, a short chip that went right between Eddy and Brock and landed in a patch of empty space. Aron burst forward, splitting the two defenders, following his pass to himself. Brock knew what he was trying to do and wedged inside, giving him a hard and fair shoulder charge that would have leveled most players.

But Aron was a tank. He churned those thick legs forward, used his muscular upper body to stand up to Brock's charge, and bounced off Eddy after that. It was a close battle, but Aron squeezed through them and reached the ball before our defenders could recover.

Riley had started to race over but he was too late. Aron dribbled straight towards the goal, just steps from the end line, as JoJo came out to cut off his angle. I thought Aron would pass the ball to one of his teammates rushing into the penalty box. Instead, Aron took one more dribble and blasted a shot to the near post. JoJo had it covered but the shot was so hard, and from such a close distance, that it deflected off her hand, hit the side post, and bounced into the goal.

Whoa, I said to myself again as Aron wagged a finger in the air and jogged upfield. *That was legit.*

From the sideline, Samantha clapped and called out "Well done!" to Aron, while Coach Beppe patted his belly and grinned at no one in particular.

When the game restarted, John kicked off to Patrick, who made a short run, got into trouble, and passed back to Otto. The two of us worked it around the midfield, getting to know each other again, and involved Caden as well. Caden was even more tanned and blond-haired than usual, as if he'd spent all his free time at the pool. He looked a little winded, out of shape from the break, but he sent a nice ball to me through two defenders.

I collected the ball near the center circle. Logan stepped up to challenge me, shaggy brown hair flying, sweat beading on his pimply face and bony arms. In the corner of my eye, I noticed Otto making a run on my left. I slipped him a pass, ran around Logan, and called for the ball again.

Otto hit me in stride. I let the ball roll through my legs, fooling their left back, then turned and made a run deep into enemy territory. The center back for the second team charged forward to stop me. I cut hard to the right, buying some space but taking myself away from the goal. That was okay. I had another plan in mind. As the center back closed me down, I took one more dribble towards the end line, turned my hips, and whipped a pass across the penalty box, waist-high and hard, knowing where Patrick liked to patrol.

And he was there.

The defense tried to shift, but Patrick was already in motion, flying through the air like a red-headed spear, going for a diving header. He made good contact ten feet from the goal and headed the ball onto the goal line, where it skipped past our new second-string keeper and into the net.

"Luckabuckaluckabucka!" Patrick cried, racing over to slap hands with me. John and Otto congratulated me as well, and it felt like we had picked up right where we left off, fitting together like the pieces of a puzzle.

You might think this was just a scrimmage, a light-hearted practice game on our first day back. And it was supposed to be.

But it quickly turned into something more. The second team was giving us a real game. They were no slouches, remember. Every single one of them had made the roster of a youth Premier League team. Logan was an excellent player and had started every game under Coach Purcell. He was playing really hard today, as intense as I'd ever seen him. Some of the other players were almost as good, and always challenging us first-teamers for our positions.

Aron, though, was on another level. A game changer. He scored another goal within minutes, this time a header off a corner kick, proving he could play in the air as well as on the ground.

Again we evened the score, after John made a beautiful goal off a pass from Eddy.

It stayed tied for a while, but right before halftime, Aron scored *again*. Samantha awarded him a penalty after a foul from Riley, and Aron smashed the free kick into the bottom left corner, just past Jojo's fingertips.

At halftime, the rain finally let up. I huddled with the other first-teamers and debated our strategy for the second half. Aron already had a hat trick. We had to do something about that.

"I'll shut him down this time," Brock said with a growl. "He's good, but I'm ready now."

Jojo snarled and pounded a fist into her palm. "Me too." Over the break, she had dyed her short hair purple and purchased a pair of black goalie pants with silver lightning bolts down the sides. "He's not getting the near post again."

A whistle blew. We saw Coach Beppe waving us over. Hoping he would dissect our play in the first half and offer some pointers, we gathered around him, noticing that he was staring at something on the ground. The rain had stopped, the clouds had parted, and a ray of sunlight had emerged. He knelt on the wet grass and motioned for us to join him. As I took a knee, I realized he was watching a little black and yellow honeybee suck nectar from a wildflower.

"You're doing well out there," he said. "I can tell you enjoy playing with each other and that is very important. The skills, *sí*, they will come. We will work on that."

What did he mean, *the skills will come?* Were we that bad? Or was he just used to coaching global superstars?

Coach Beppe knelt beside the creature. "Behold the humble honeybee. The most advanced insect on the planet, and one which has many lessons for us. They can sense a storm long before it arrives and can beat their wings so fast they create their own magnetic field, which they use to collect pollen, like a magnet attracting iron. Bees are also the only insects that provide food for humans. Well, some people eat ants and beetles, but that is different. Bees *make* honey, and it never spoils." Coach held out his left hand beside the bee and let it crawl onto his open palm. "These magnificent creatures have the most complex language in the insect world, more advanced than many animals. Nor do they have to shout to understand each other. They communicate with subtle body movements. Wiggles and waggles and woggles. They sense, observe, and gesture."

Coach Beppe held out a finger on his other hand to the bee, causing some of us to gasp, thinking it would sting him. But the tiny bee crawled on his finger and wriggled in place, as if happy to see a friend. "There are many other superpowers that bees have. But most of all, we must envy the way they work together. Each bee in the hive has a defined task. They build their homes in unison and make honey. They keep each other warm, care for the sick, and search for food. Everything they do is a carefully conducted orchestra we are only beginning to understand. Every team should play like the bees. Now," he said, shooing the insect into the air and pushing to his feet, "go finish the game!"

After exchanging looks of pure confusion, we all ran back to start the second half, wondering if our new coach had been kidnapped and replaced by an alien.

On my way to my position as a number 10—center attacking mid, with Otto and Caden behind me on either side—I found myself jogging out next to Aron.

"Nice playing," I said.

"Thanks," he replied with a slight accent, then ran off without returning the compliment.

Almost as if I was a fan who had just asked for an autograph.

"Three to two," Samantha called out after placing the ball on the half line. "Let's see what you've got, Knights!"

Since Coach Purcell had left, our first team had never been down to the second team. When the whistle blew, we pressed them hard, and evened the score with an impressive long-range blast from Otto.

The cloud cover returned. It started to rain again. Back and forth the game went, with both sides narrowly missing chances. Whenever Aron made a run, Brock and Eddy double-teamed him, or Riley sprinted over to help out. JoJo made a few amazing saves, including stopping another one of Aron's rockets towards the near post.

We were playing a full-length game. As the time wound down, Aron grew more and more frustrated, calling for the ball every time one of his teammates touched it. I could tell how badly he wanted to win, and I was happy he was so good, because he could really help us.

But I didn't like the way he was treating his teammates.

The next time the second team took the ball down the right side, I crept back, waiting for someone to pass to Aron. Logan finally did, and I left my position to sprint back and help on defense.

Aron received the ball in the corner, with Eddy guarding him. Brock was hovering near the penalty box, wary of committing too soon. Aron held Eddy off with an arm and spun around him, a nifty move that opened up some space.

Except I happened to be waiting. I took Aron by surprise and stripped the ball. He rushed me, and I danced around him, evading his attempts to win the ball back. I heard him yelling in frustration as I pressed upfield and left him scrambling in the wet grass.

"Leo!" Patrick called out from higher up the field.

He was too far away. I sent the ball to Otto instead and ran ahead to help with the counterattack. Otto got the ball to Patrick, who tried to probe the defense but didn't have an opening. He was forced to pull back and return the ball to Otto.

I was still racing upfield. As always, Otto could sense what I was doing, and led me with a pass right in the heart of the defense. With my first touch, I sent the ball a few feet forward instead of trapping it, evading a defender in the process. Now I had a clear shot on goal. I reared back for the shot, knowing I had a good angle and an excellent chance to score.

Before I could take the shot, someone tackled me from behind, a hard but fair challenge. I fell to the ground. After taking a moment to recover, I looked over to see who had stopped me.

It was Aron. He must have left his position and sprinted all the way upfield to make that tackle.

Without a word, or offering me a hand, he brushed grass off his shorts and rejoined the play.

Seconds later, just before the final whistle blew, John scored another goal off a rebound in the penalty box.

We had won the game, but it was far closer than any of us expected.

Exhausted and muddy and soaking wet, I trudged off the field, thinking how Aron had an attitude problem and an ego like Jackson, the kid who had just moved to my hometown. The only difference was that Aron could back it up.

Our new recruit was as good as advertised.

But was he going to help our team or pull us apart?

ENTRY #5

Final Preparations

That was our hardest practice of the week. With the tourney only a few days away, our coaches didn't want to exhaust our legs.

Samantha moved Aron to the first team for the other scrimmages. We played half games and destroyed the second team.

Under Coach Beppe, we continued to practice drills that focused on the fusilli. He even transferred the lessons into short-sided games and set pieces. None of us really knew what it was all about, though I knew one thing for sure: I would never forget the shape of that kind of pasta.

He also continued to preach how we needed to work together on the field like the honeybees. At least we understood the point of the lesson, if not how to carry it out.

By the end of the week, despite the strange practices, I started to believe we might have a fighting chance in the tournament. Aron definitely made us stronger. He provided a goal-scoring threat on the right wing that we had been missing. JoJo continued to improve, and Riley grew more and more comfortable on defense.

We still had plenty of weaknesses, but so does every team.

At least I hoped.

During dinner in the cafeteria on Friday night, Samantha

and Coach Luca said their goodbyes and wished us luck, telling us they would be closely following our progress. Another manager handed all of the players a tournament swag bag that Sami's father (Mr. Haddad) had paid for. We dug into the bags right then and there, pulling out special uniforms that had black-and-silver stripes and our last names and numbers in bright orange lettering. The swag bag also contained game shorts, socks, shin guards, a ball with the Tournament of Champions logo, and even a brand-new pair of cleats.

I loved my new jersey right away and sucked in a breath when I saw the number on the back.

For the first time in my life, I was officially a 10.

You can't switch numbers during the regular season, but that rule doesn't apply to a summer tournament, and Samantha wanted our jerseys to reflect our positions. She had already posted the new numbers, so it wasn't a surprise, but it hadn't seemed real until I was holding my jersey in my hands. I snuck a glance at Caden and saw him quietly staring at the number 8 on his own uniform. I hoped he wasn't taking it too hard. I had thought I was a number 9 for my entire life, until Samantha convinced me to make the switch—and that had worked out for me.

When Coach Beppe dismissed us, he ordered us to bed early, since we were leaving for France in the morning. I was excited about the trip and couldn't wait to get going.

⚽ ⚽ ⚽

Back in my room, before I turned out the lights, I heard a knock at the door. Wondering which of my friends had stopped by, I opened the door and found Tig standing in the hallway. He was dressed in stylish jeans, white slip-on shoes, and a purple T-shirt.

"Boss! Glad I caught you. Samantha and I are going out, and I wanted to say good luck in the tournament. You excited?"

"Definitely."

"You should be. It's going to be an incredible experience. I only played in it once."

"Did you win?"

"We finished third. That's the best a Dragons youth team has ever finished. Playing in Europe is tough."

"Isn't England in Europe?"

He chuckled. "Yeah, but that's how the English talk about the big competitions on the continent, like the Champions League and the Europa League. It's a different experience from the Premier League. You'll see new styles and gobs of talent." He chucked me on the shoulder. "It's still soccer, though, hey? You be you, and everything will be fine."

"I hope so," I muttered, thinking about what he had said. *Third place was the best the London Dragons have ever finished.*

"I heard about the new coach," Tig said. "Beppe's a legend. How is it so far?"

"He's . . . nice." I shuddered, remembering the start to last season. "Not at all like Coach Purcell. But Coach Beppe, um, well, he's not what I expected."

"Yeah, I've heard his practices are a little unusual."

"So far, I've learned that all we have to do is play like honeybees flying through a field full of pasta."

Tig blinked. "How's that, boss?"

I laughed at my own joke. "Maybe the lessons will get easier to understand."

"Anyway, knock 'em dead. Samantha is torn up she can't go. We'll be rooting for you."

"Can you do that? As a Dragon?"

He flashed a grin. "We're both Premier League players, right? It's good for all of us when a team does well abroad."

I thought about that, felt a tingle of pride, and then asked him something that had been on my mind. "Hey Tig, are you a pro?"

"Eh? Whatcha mean?"

"I mean, do you get paid to play on the U21s? Or do only the adult Premier League players make money?"

"Hmm. It's a good question. The answer isn't so easy, though." He leaned an arm against the side of the doorway and fiddled with a leather bracelet on his wrist. "In England, you can't earn a salary until you're seventeen. So under that definition, that's when you can turn pro."

"Are there any seventeen-year-olds in the Premier League?"

"Doubtful. I'd have to check. Maybe one or two got called up last season, but they weren't regulars. Technically, you can play when you're even younger. A few years back, Arsenal put a fifteen-year-old in a game."

I was shocked. "Really?"

"That's an extreme example. They had a lot of injuries at the time. That player was the youngest ever in a Premier League game."

"Do you think I need an agent?"

Tig smiled. "Not yet, boss. You can't sign until you turn sixteen. Stick with me and Samantha for now, we'll watch out for you."

"Thanks," I said, and truly meant it.

"Back to your question, though. Like I said, you can't earn a pro salary until you turn seventeen. But clubs can offer you a schollie—that's a scholarship—even earlier."

"Don't I already have a scholarship?"

"Yeah, but it's not the same. Every team does it a little differently at your age, but you're getting room and board for school. Sort of like a scholarship to a private school back home, for good grades or to play a sport. But clubs can offer you a *professional* scholarship that pays wages once you turn sixteen."

"Oh. Like how much?"

"Minimal. A few thousand a year. But it's a commitment, and it means the club is serious about you. A scholarship is extremely hard to get, and it's often the turning point in a player's career. So, for most of us, 'going pro' means getting an academy scholarship by the end of the U16 season. That's a very important time in your soccer journey. Getting a schollie still isn't the Premier League, but you're on your way, and getting paid to play soccer."

"I think I understand."

Tig gave me a long look. "Now you know the deal. Knowledge is power, Leo. At some point, you'll need to understand contracts and money almost as well as you do soccer, so people can't take advantage of you. But listen, hey? I don't want you worrying about all that yet. Nothing good can come of stressing about turning pro at your age. Got it?"

If my dad had told me that, or any of my coaches, except maybe Samantha, I probably wouldn't have listened.

But when Tig told me something, I knew he was being real. "All right," I said. "I promise I won't think *too* much about it."

He chuckled and gave me a fist bump. "Deal."

After he left, I lay in bed thinking about everything he had said. Now I understood the journey to becoming a professional soccer player a little better. Though my ultimate goal still seemed as far away as the moon and stars, if I played well and continued to grow and train, maybe one day I would earn a ticket on a rocket ship.

ENTRY #6

Paris!

Early the next morning, our team, along with Coach Beppe and a physical trainer and two managers, took a bus from Lewisham to the St. Pancras railway station in north London. The St. Pancras station is so old and big I thought it was a castle when I first saw it. The red brick building even has a clock tower that's almost as impressive as Big Ben.

Inside the station, I looked around in awe at the hordes of people and the rounded glass ceiling high overhead. A digital board announced when trains would depart to cities all over Britain and to other countries in Europe. You might be wondering how taking a train to other countries is possible, since England is on an island. And the last time I checked, trains don't swim.

But trains do go through tunnels, and that's how we'd be traveling to Paris: through a thirty-one-mile tunnel that goes all the way beneath the English Channel, the body of water separating England from France.

After a passport check, our team piled into a Eurostar train with hundreds of other people. I had never traveled by train, and it was much nicer than I expected. There were snack bars and bathrooms and plenty of room to sit and stand. Most of the seats were arranged in groups of four, with two seats side by side, facing another pair of seats across a little table. I sat next to John, while Otto and Eddy took the seats across from us.

The train pulled smoothly out of the station, much different from the rocking motion of the subway. I wish I could tell you that I saw the Eurostar train plunge like a roller coaster straight down a tunnel beneath the sea, staring up at whales and sharks and giant squid through a glass ceiling, but that wasn't the case. When we reached the coast, I didn't even notice we were entering a tunnel until I looked over and saw darkness outside the windows instead of the gray English sky. Still, it was exciting to think we were traveling deep underground, beneath all that water, on a high-speed train.

Not far away, Logan and Caden were sitting next to each other. Caden was listening to headphones with his arms crossed, and Logan was popping his pimples, as usual. Half the players on the team had as many pimples as Logan, but he loved to squeeze the gunk out and flick it away. I think he just enjoyed grossing people out. I heard from John, who knew those two a little better because they had played together longer, that Caden's parents were getting a divorce. I had noticed Caden seemed quieter than usual, and not nearly as cocky, even before Samantha changed his jersey number.

Logan, on the other hand, seemed way more chill than last season. After losing his starting position, I worried he would grow bitter, but instead he had become a leader of the second team, even drawing praise for his good attitude.

Across from them were Patrick and Sami. Oddly, they had become close friends, despite being opposites. Off the field, Sami liked to wear boring button-down shirts, while Patrick chose T-shirts that matched his personality: loud and colorful and funny. Sami was short and squat; Patrick was thin and lanky. Sami didn't seem to mind that Patrick was often the center of attention and talked nonstop. In fact, since Sami was so shy, I think he enjoyed being lost in Patrick's shadow.

In the row behind us, Brock and Riley were sitting together, if you can believe that. I don't think I would call them friends, but they were no longer enemies. When they talked to each other, it was usually in the form of an argument, often about whether London or Manchester was a better city, whose accent was harder to understand, or if Manchester United—Riley's team—was better than Liverpool, who Brock supported.

If you're wondering what professional team—besides Lewisham, of course—everyone else rooted for, well, John was a diehard Arsenal fan, Caden supported Chelsea, Otto liked Bayern Munich, and Eddy rooted for Real Madrid. Sami loved Manchester City, Patrick claimed allegiance to Juventus for some reason, and Logan followed Tottenham.

Everyone loved their national team, me included. Even in the Premier League, I liked to root for teams with players from the United States. I also loved Barcelona because, well, they're Barcelona. When I think of them, I always think of Messi, even though he's moved on.

A little farther down the train, Aron and JoJo had the bad luck of sitting next to Coach Beppe and a stranger. Not that Coach Beppe was unpleasant or anything—as I've said, he's very nice—but who wants to sit next to the coach on a road trip? The rest of us were cutting up or playing cards or listening to music. Aron and JoJo had their backs to each other and were trying to sleep.

Patrick had switched seats with Eddy so Patrick could play

chess with Otto on a little magnetic board Otto carried with him to away games. John and I chatted as we watched them play. Eventually our conversation turned to the Tournament of Champions and our first game against Paris Saint-Martin.

John leaned back in his seat and interlaced his fingers behind his head. "So, what's the action, bruvs? We have to take it to the Frenchies."

Patrick looked up from his game and shot two fake arrows at the ceiling. This had become his signature move, even though he had received a red card in the game when he'd started it.

We all knew what he meant.

Paris Saint-Martin was a target in our sights.

I said, "I hope Coach Beppe has a good strategy."

"I wouldn't count on that," John said. "Don't you think he would have told us by now?"

"I bet we'll hear the game plan tonight. He has to tell us *something*. Maybe he needs to study up on them. He's used to the pros, not youth teams."

"Hey hey, I think he's studying insects and Italian food."

I turned to Otto, knowing how much research he did on teams, players, and soccer tactics. "What do you know about this team? They have to have some flaws."

"Not really," my Hungarian friend said matter-of-factly as he moved his queen across the board. "They're the number one U14 team in Europe for a reason. They have top players at every position."

John shook his head. "No one's invincible. Not even super-heroes. Wolverine hates magnets, Superman has kryptonite, and Thor needs his hammer."

"Exactly," I said. "Everyone is beatable. And we have top players too."

"Have you seen Paris Saint-Martin play?" Otto said. "I have, and they're extremely impressive."

I waved a hand, annoyed by his attitude. "It's almost like you've already decided we're going to lose."

"Not at all," he said. "I'm just practical." He moved his queen again, this time right in front of his opponent's king. "Checkmate."

Patrick studied the board, ran a hand through his wild red hair, and sighed. "Luckabucka green grass goo. Otto, I hate you."

⚽ ⚽ ⚽

Two hours after leaving St. Pancras, we arrived at station Gare du Nord in Paris, France.

Just like that, we were in another country. It's so easy to travel in Europe.

The station was even busier than St. Pancras. In fact, Coach Beppe told us that Gare du Nord was the busiest train station in all of Europe, and, except for Japan, the entire world!

We took the Paris Metro—that's what the subway is called here—from right inside the station. It was a short journey to République, the closest stop to our hotel. The Metro was fun, but all the announcements were in French, so none of us had any idea what they were saying.

When we emerged, the weather was very different from England. The sun was shining, and it was scorching hot outside. As hot and humid as Ohio at this time of year.

République is a busy outdoor square with a statue of a

woman atop a large stone monument in the center. There were lots of trees, people playing soccer and frisbee, and shops and restaurants surrounding the square. Our hotel was a short walk away. When we arrived, I learned I was sharing a room with John and Eddy. The room had no air conditioning and three single beds squeezed into a tiny space. But who cared? We were in Paris!

After dropping our bags, we met everyone in the lobby, and Coach Beppe gathered us around him.

"I hope everyone had a pleasant journey," he said. "I'm sure you're all eager to see Paris. Has anyone been before?"

Only Otto and Aron raised their hands.

"*Bueno, bueno.* The City of Lights is one of my favorites. I will be your tour guide for our stay. Now, you've all seen the schedule for the tournament, and you know the games in the group stage are only a few days apart. I suppose young legs do not need as much rest. This doesn't leave us much time, but, at each stop, we'll see a few sights and make time for a special football outing I have prepared."

"Whatcha mean?" JoJo said brashly. "What kinda outing?"

Coach Beppe gave a mysterious smile. "Ah, but you will see very soon."

⚽ ⚽ ⚽

After leaving the hotel, we walked along Canal Saint-Martin, which was only two blocks away. The canal was emerald green and had cafes and restaurants along the banks. Lots of young people were strolling near the water, sitting on blankets in the sun, and walking across footbridges that spanned the canal.

We returned to République, where Coach Beppe took us

to a street vendor who made crepes right in front of our eyes. Crepes are like thin little pancakes with different toppings. I had a chocolate crepe that was delicious and was going on my favorite food list.

After that, we walked through the Marais district, an area full of fancy restaurants and buildings that Coach Beppe and the managers couldn't stop talking about but which seemed like regular old buildings to me. I mean, fine, they're all historic and nice looking, but they're still just buildings.

Let me stop and say something here. As soon as we arrived in Paris, and especially on this walk, it really hit me that I was in a foreign country. When I first arrived in London, I had the same feeling, and it was exciting, but I never thought I would have it again, because that was my first time overseas. But Paris is completely different from London, so I felt amazed and impressed all over again.

Something else. Traveling in England is one thing, where everyone speaks English, but traveling in France, where almost no one speaks your language, is like leveling up in a video game. It's more challenging and a little disorienting. I can't understand anyone on the street or read any of the signs. But that's okay. It's also exciting. As I wandered around and took it all in, I realized I loved exploring foreign cities and being in a completely different place.

John and Eddy were seeing Paris for the first time and enjoying it like me. But not everyone felt the same. Brock couldn't stop talking about how weird everything was. He made fun of the way people dressed and talked and kept grumbling about the lack of fish and chips.

Riley was in a state of constant confusion, walking around

with his mouth open, muttering incomprehensible phrases beneath his breath. I wasn't sure if he liked Paris or not.

JoJo looked unimpressed by anything we had seen. She hadn't removed her headphones since we arrived.

Patrick was asking people on the street silly questions in his thick Irish accent, just to see the confusion on their faces.

To my surprise, Logan was hanging out with some of the second-team players, leaving Caden by himself, lost in his thoughts. When I tried to talk to Caden, he said he was tired, then crossed to the other side of the street.

Aron was walking alone, too, though he seemed content with his own company, instead of sad like Caden or sullen like JoJo.

⚽ ⚽ ⚽

When we reached a Metro station, Coach Beppe announced we only had two stops left in the day. I jumped on the train with my friends, laughing and chatting, not really paying attention to how many stops we traveled.

When we finally exited the train and stepped outside into the bright sun in a crowd of people, Brock said, "Where are we now? There better be some chips around here. And not those skinny French things."

In response, Coach Beppe pointed a finger overhead. I craned my neck and gasped when I saw a curved iron tower soaring high into the blue sky, almost right above our heads, so wide at the base I hadn't even realized we were standing so close to it.

Coach Beppe held up a palm. "Welcome to the Eiffel Tower."

The tower had four massive legs connected to a spire which narrowed to a point at the top. My teammates and I, along with all the other people clustered like ants beneath the tower, couldn't seem to stop staring. The soaring monument was the most stunning sight I had ever seen.

"Whoa," John said. "That's dope."

Riley seemed unable to process the Eiffel Tower, his narrow head cocked to the side and his mouth slack, as if he had just seen a pig fly through the sky. "Big," he said. "Really really big."

"One thousand and eighty-three feet, to be exact," Otto added. "It used to be the tallest building on Earth. It has a secret apartment too."

"Chips!" Brock said, angling towards a street vendor with a British flag flapping above the cart. He wasn't even looking at the Eiffel Tower. "Finally!"

Coach Beppe let us hang out in the park and cross the street to walk along the river, which provided even better views. Eventually he herded us like sheep onto the Metro again, and we took a longer journey to a stop called Anvers.

After exiting, we walked up a hill along a cobblestone street lined with old shops and markets. This part of the city, Montmartre, was leafy green and felt like a little village in the heart of Paris. After climbing through a park, up and up and up, we emerged at the base of a medieval church called Sacré-Coeur. To reach the church, there were even more steps to climb, and by the time we reached the top, Coach Beppe was huffing and puffing.

I heard dance music to my left, turned, and saw a crowd of people watching a man in shorts and a tank top juggling a soccer ball on top of a low wall. Behind him, we could see far across the city, all the way to the Eiffel Tower in the distance. It seemed like all of Paris, the entire world, was at our feet.

Coach Beppe clapped his hands. "Ah, here we are. Right on time for practice."

"Practice?" Riley said, throwing up his pale, skinny arms. "Wut?"

Our coach urged us forward, into the crowd watching the man juggling on the wall. Some of the bystanders were shouting encouragement and clapping to the beat of the music blasting out of a speaker. The soccer player looked about thirty and had Tig's walnut skin tone, though he was shorter and more muscular.

He was also an incredible juggler, even better than Tig. I couldn't believe what I was seeing. Atop that narrow ledge, the man was doing all kinds of tricks: shoulder stalls, 360s, different kinds of around-the-worlds, and plenty of moves I had never seen before. He even added gymnastics to the routine, such as one-armed handstands and headstands with the ball balanced on top of his feet. Once I caught my breath as he kicked the ball high, did a back flip, and resumed juggling when he landed.

Whoa, I thought. *Surely this guy is a pro? Or used to be?*

People in the crowd were walking up to drop coins in a bucket at the base of the wall. The man kept juggling for another song, not once dropping the ball, before he bowed to the crowd, hopped down, collected the tips, and walked away holding his ball under his arm.

"That's the lesson?" I said. "Impressive."

Coach Beppe grinned. "The first part, yes. Now it's your turn."

"Me?"

"All of you. Try it out. I urge you to be careful, no handstands or flips please. We do not want a twisted ankle or a bump on a head." Coach Beppe shrugged out of his backpack and took out a ball. "Let's see how you do. Who would like to go first?"

"Leo," John said with his infectious laugh, slapping me on the back. "He's the best trickster."

The team started to chant my name. I had no choice but to jump on the wall. Coach Beppe lifted the ball in the air, and I caught it on my thigh and began to juggle. John put a rap tune on his phone and turned up the volume. Most of the onlookers had left, but I still felt awkward and embarrassed.

The wall was not very high, but it was narrow, and I could barely move without risking a fall. I juggled in place to get my balance, using my feet and thighs and chest. When I flicked the ball to my head, it got more difficult. I tried a back heel and dropped the ball, afraid I would slip. My teammates groaned in dismay.

"You think you can do better?" Coach Beppe said. "We shall see."

John went next, and then Eddy, followed by the rest of the team. The more we roasted each other, the harder it was to concentrate and stay on the wall.

"That was a nice warmup," Coach Beppe said. "Shall we try another time? Leo?"

"Sure," I said, and hopped back up.

This time Coach Beppe took off his ball cap, turned it upside down, and set it on the wall close to my feet. "Let us see if you can earn your keep like the professionals. Gather around, everyone!" he shouted. "The exhibition is about to begin!"

So far, no one had been paying much attention to us, but now a small crowd started to gather. They were all watching me, and I got even more nervous. I hadn't signed up for this! Before I could change my mind, Coach Beppe tossed the ball to me. Feeling pressure to do something interesting for all the people watching, I caught the ball on my instep, lifted it high in the air, and trapped it between my shoulder blades. A few cries of approval arose from the crowd. People began to clap, and I began to juggle, getting more and more fancy—right until an older teenager shouted something in French from the front row, causing me to look up and drop the ball.

My teammates hooted and whistled as I hopped off the wall, humiliated.

"We must learn to tune out distractions," Coach Beppe said. "Next!"

One by one, everyone on the team got on the wall again, but no one lasted long in the spotlight. The group of older teens knew we did not have the skill or laser focus of the man who had gone before us, and they seemed to enjoy taunting us. Every time they shouted or waved their hands, it broke someone's attention.

Riley dropped the ball almost as soon as he began juggling. When the crowd roared with delight, he sneered and shook a fist.

"Tsk tsk," Coach Beppe said. "If you cannot handle this, how can you handle fifty thousand screaming fans at a rival stadium? You must learn to control your emotions."

Eddy did a little dance routine while he juggled, and Patrick made everyone laugh by pretending to fall constantly, lurching back and forth on the ledge while somehow keeping the ball in the air.

But neither lasted very long. When it was my turn again, determined to do better, I jumped on the wall as the crowd clapped in approval. The older teens started to jeer and wave their arms, determined to break my concentration. I tried to block them out and focus, letting the ball become the center of my universe. I loved to juggle and decided to try a reverse toe bounce. Normally that's an easy one for me, and I hopped up to swing my leg around, like I had done a thousand times before. But this time, when I landed, only the front of my foot touched down on the wall. I felt nothing but air under my heel, causing me to wobble, lose my balance, and fall backwards.

With nothing wounded except my pride, I climbed back over the wall as the older teens roared with delight. A few people, mostly parents with small children, dropped a few consolation coins into Coach Beppe's hat.

"You must be aware of your surroundings at all times," Coach Beppe said as I returned to the team. "Focus, awareness, control. That is the lesson."

By this time, the expert juggler had returned. I watched his routine again, even more in awe than before. I knew I was being hard on myself, but I walked away feeling as if I had failed. Why had I been so nervous up there?

It was time for a tour of Sacré-Coeur. On the way inside the cathedral, Coach Beppe knelt in front of an old woman begging at the entrance. He took the hat with the loose change we had earned and dumped all the money in her bowl.

"Wut?" Riley said. "I almost died for that!"

Coach Beppe chuckled and shooed us inside the church. After walking around inside—there was lots of marble and gold and fancy paintings, none of which interested me in the slightest—we returned outside and realized the sun had set. In the distance, I saw the Eiffel Tower lit up with golden lights, shining high above the city. It was even better at night than during the day.

Eventually we gathered by the wall to begin the long descent to the Metro. When Coach Beppe did a headcount, he realized someone was missing. I looked back and saw JoJo standing alone at the top of the steps near the entrance to Sacré-Coeur, her headphones slung around her neck instead of on her head, staring in silence at the Eiffel Tower.

ENTRY #7

Game Time!

We woke the next morning with one thing on our minds.

Our first game in the Tournament of Champions.

In just a few short hours, at noon Paris time, we were set to take on the number one U14 club team not just in the tournament but in all of Europe.

We had breakfast in the hotel. Everyone was in good spirits, ready to play. Even Aron joined in, sitting with the rest of us for once and describing his life in Switzerland. His father had played professional soccer, and his mother was a champion skier. At age nine, Aron had joined the top academy in his country. I wondered if he had ever had a doubt or worry in his entire life. He probably got his hair cut by an Olympic hair stylist and shopped for groceries at the world's best supermarket.

As we ate, Coach Beppe told us we'd be keeping the same formation—a 4–3–3—as well as the same starting lineup we'd been using in practice. Nothing had changed from the end of last season except Aron had replaced Ajay.

"What about Paris Saint-Martin?" Otto asked.

Coach Beppe picked up a croissant. "What about them?"

"I know they use a 4–2–3–1. How should we play against it?"

Coach Beppe took a bite of the croissant, chewed slowly,

swallowed, and wiped his mouth with a napkin. "Let me pose a question. What if I give you a detailed game plan, something different than what we've used before, and the coach of Paris Saint-Martin decides to use a new formation? What then? We will have prepared for nothing. Play your game, the best you can play it, and let them react to you."

"But what about their striker, Theo?" Otto persisted. "He scored twenty-seven goals last season."

"Then I suggest you guard him closely, *sí*?"

⚽   ⚽   ⚽

Before breakfast, we had all left our duffel bags in the lobby, under the watchful eye of the receptionist. On our way out, we each grabbed our bags, slung them over our shoulders, and stepped through the automatic hotel doors and into the warm morning air.

A charter bus was parked on the curb. The Paris Saint-Martin Academy was a short ride away. Within minutes we were stepping off the bus and following Coach Beppe and the managers through a tall wooden gate into a soccer complex just as impressive as any of the Premier League academies.

We proceeded to the visitors' locker room, where we dropped our bags and began to dress. In case you're wondering, JoJo, like Samantha, dressed in a separate room and returned once we'd all changed clothes.

I was already wearing my game shorts and socks. I opened my duffel bag and pulled out my shin guards, cleats, and . . . wait. Where was my jersey?

Huh. I knew I had packed it. Right before breakfast, I had stuck it in my bag on my way out of my room, as I did before every game. I always put it right on top, so it would be easy to access, but it must have fallen to the bottom.

I pawed through the bag again, taking everything out and setting it on the bench.

No jersey.

How could this be?

Confused and ashamed, wondering if the coach had a spare jersey or would bench me for being irresponsible, I looked up to tell him—then saw John and Eddy digging frantically through their bags.

So were a lot of players, I realized.

"*Pamplemousse*," Patrick said. "Where's my shirt?"

Coach Beppe frowned. "Eh? What is this?" He turned to the managers, who seemed just as perplexed as we were. Only a handful of people had their jerseys, not even enough to start the game. Coach Beppe sent one of the managers racing back to the bus and ordered the rest of us to the field for warmups.

As we exited the dressing room, I saw the Paris Saint-Martin players on the field, looking smart in their red-and-white uniforms with blue trim. We were forced to warm up in our T-shirts. It was embarrassing.

Within minutes, the manager that had gone to the bus came sprinting back empty-handed across the field. We all heard him tell Coach Beppe the uniforms were nowhere to be seen.

Coach Beppe ordered him back to the hotel in a taxi.

By this time, the Paris Saint-Martin players were laughing and pointing fingers at us. Remember Javier from the Dragons' Academy? The lightning-fast winger with earrings and bright green hair? He was playing for Paris Saint-Martin and still had green hair.

Just before the game was set to start, he jogged over to me. "Leo, *bienvenue à Paris*. I see most of you are not wearing uniforms."

"That's true."

"We find this a little disrespectful, *oui*? Is this a practice game to you? When do you plan to change?"

"We, um, can't find our jerseys."

"Eh? What do you mean?"

"Just what I said. Someone took them or something."

Javier looked confused and ran off. A moment later, the referee blew his whistle and waved Coach Beppe over. We heard the ref threatening a forfeit if we didn't have uniforms.

Oh no. Would our first game in the Tournament of Champions end before it even began?

We stopped warming up and gathered in a huddle near our bench. Finally, the manager who had left in a taxi ran back onto the field, giving us a surge of hope—right before he informed Coach Beppe the uniforms were nowhere to be found.

This was terrible.

What was going on?

The referee kept checking his watch and pacing back and forth. The French coach walked over to Coach Beppe and the referee, and they huddled together. When they finished, the referee still seemed unhappy, and the French coach shouted something to his bench.

Coach Beppe walked towards us. I couldn't read his expression. Just when I began to despair, one of the French managers ran over carrying a large bag, and Coach Beppe told us the referee had agreed to let us play wearing the practice uniforms of the Paris Saint-Martin players.

Whew. For a second, I was sure we would have to forfeit. Unsure what to think—had someone stolen our uniforms?—we each tried to pick out one of the all-white shirts that fit us best. I realized the one I had selected was Javier's number eleven.

The referee shooed us onto the field. Our team lined up, trying to shake off the embarrassment of playing in our opponents' practice jerseys. This was not how I imagined starting the Tournament of Champions, but we had to get past it.

I clapped a few times to give myself energy, determined to stay positive. The whistle blew, and from that point forward, I didn't have time to think about our uniforms.

It was game on!

Paris Saint-Martin—their nickname was the Bayonets—had the ball at kickoff. As they surged forward, I realized how big they were. During warmups, they had appeared large from a distance, but I was so distracted by the missing jerseys I hadn't thought too much about it. And Javier was about my size, medium height and wiry. But most of the other Bayonets were closer to Aron and Otto and Brock's size, and a few were even taller. The striker Otto had warned us about, Theo, resembled a younger version of Mbappé and seemed almost as fast. He was a blur as he ran by me, calling for the ball. Their center midfielder noticed and lofted a high pass over our defense.

I held my breath as Riley and Brock scrambled backwards. Theo was coming on hard. JoJo started to leave the goal and then turned back, realizing she wouldn't reach the ball in time.

Theo sprinted right past Brock, shrugging off his attempt at a shoulder charge. The ball rolled all the way into the penalty box. Now it was a footrace between Riley and Theo, who had started much farther upfield. Surely the French striker couldn't make up that much ground on Riley, our fastest player, on the first push of the game?

As Riley's rattail swayed behind him, he beat Theo to the ball, but just barely, and was forced to kick it across the end line. I ran back to help defend the corner kick, feeling lost in a sea of giant players as I jostled for position in the penalty box.

The referee dropped his hand. A Bayonet winger took the kick, curving one of the hardest crosses I had ever seen into the penalty area. It whizzed past me. Incredibly, a Bayonet player leaped into the air and attempted a scissor-kick volley. I watched, stunned, as he made contact and rocketed the ball at the near post.

JoJo stood frozen in the center of the goal. She had no chance to save it. Just before the shot crossed the goal line, Brock threw his body in front of the ball, letting it bounce off his chest. I winced, thinking how that cannonball might have caved in my stomach. But Brock didn't even flinch. When the ball hit the ground, he kicked it high in the air, threw his fists up, and roared like a wild animal.

"Let's go, Knights!"

His roar gave me a burst of adrenaline. I raced toward the ball, which was bouncing towards the center circle. One of the Bayonet defenders reached it first and tried a one-touch pass to Javier, who was playing on the right wing but not too high. I knew that in a 4–2–3–1 formation, the striker stayed deep in enemy territory, while the wingers had the freedom to drift back to midfield or make runs down the line.

Javier ran to receive the ball. I stepped in front of him,

stole the ball, and dribbled into a pocket of space. As he scrambled to catch up, I was off and running, searching for my teammates. Patrick and John were lagging behind, but Aron was racing down the wing, calling for the ball.

Why not? It was a long pass, and he was covered by a defender, but I decided to give it a shot and see what he could do.

My pass soared over the Bayonets' defense and landed at Aron's feet. His defender was breathing down his neck, but Aron coolly trapped the ball with a perfect first touch. He feigned a pass to the middle then kicked the ball down the wing and took off.

His defender was very quick and stayed with him. It was a battle of two warriors, shoulder to shoulder, Aron trying to gain a step so he could cross the ball, his defender battling to contain him. In the end, Aron got the upper hand, and managed to send a low arcing cross to the outer edge of the penalty box.

I had kept running. Otto and John caught up with me. I chested Aron's pass to Otto, who used a back heel to flick it to John, who took a one-touch shot on goal, top right corner.

The French goalie dove and saved it.

We hadn't scored, but I liked the way the game had started.

Their goalie rolled the ball out to one of their center backs, a tall player with legs like flagpoles and the name Gaston on his jersey. He took two dribbles and crushed the ball upfield, again to Javier. As my green-haired friend trapped the ball, Eddy stepped up to challenge him. I knew Javier had sick moves, and winced as he used a nasty stepover to blow by Eddy.

Brock slid over to help. Instead of driving deeper into the corner, Javier surprised everyone by cutting hard inside, behind Brock, and launching a left-footed missile at the far post. It was a long shot but very well hit. I cringed as the ball screamed towards the net. JoJo eyed the shot, took a few quick steps to her right, leaped up, caught the ball in midair, and landed hard on her side.

Normally JoJo punched or slapped the ball away, but she had caught that one, making sure we kept possession. Impressive.

Sami ran over to help her up, but she brushed him aside and threw a long ball to Caden. She was getting better at her long passes too. With a defender on Caden's heels, instead of trying to turn, he played it safe and passed back to Sami.

A winger twice Sami's size sprinted towards him, pressuring the ball. Sami stayed calm, took a step to his right, and chipped the ball to Aron down the line. The pass was a little short, and Aron had to come back to receive it. By the time he arrived, a defender had stepped in and stolen the ball.

Aron flung out a hand. "Too short! Lead me next time!"

Sami looked stung by his words, but I was already on my heels, trying to defend the counterattack. Caden missed a slide tackle, forcing me to come over and challenge the dribbler. The Bayonet midfielder tried to spin around me. I stayed with him. He kept dancing, feinting this way and that, but couldn't shake me. Frustrated, he passed to another midfielder, but Otto read the play and intercepted the ball.

Sometimes my Hungarian friend had eyes in the back of his head. Without looking up, he turned and sent an amazing long pass to Patrick. The ball rolled down the wing, a cherry ready to be plucked off the stem. Patrick sprinted towards it. All he had to do was reach it first, and he had a clear path to goal.

Normally, in this situation, Patrick beat his defender. He had a quick first step and was always in good position.

But the French fullback was a speedster. He overtook Patrick from behind, turned with the ball, and sent a pass downfield even better than Otto's. Javier let the ball roll through his legs, fooling Eddy once again, and sprinted down the sideline.

Everyone raced back as Javier sent a cross whipping into the middle of our defense. Brock and Riley tried to sandwich Theo, but the French striker trapped the ball with his chest and, without letting the ball touch the ground, fired a volley that ripped into the back of the net.

Just like that, we were down a goal.

The game went back and forth until just before halftime, when the Bayonets held possession for so long you just felt they were going to score.

And they did. One of their fullbacks took a long range shot from thirty yards out that dipped and bobbed and caught everyone, including JoJo, off guard. I don't think she or any of us had ever seen a shot that hard from that far out. The fullback who scored was as big as a U16 player.

At the halftime whistle, the Bayonets jogged off the field, relaxed and confident. My teammates looked as exhausted as I felt. I followed them slowly to the sideline, the June sun beating down on my back, sweat dripping down my face and arms. We had given them everything we had and kept it close for a time. It was a respectable performance against the top-ranked team in the tournament.

But we were still losing 2–0.

"Okay," Coach Beppe said as we collapsed on the locker room benches with our water bottles. "I think you played well, *sí*, except for a few moments of inattention. You must always keep your focus. And move more around the field." He waved his hands in the air in a complicated pattern. "Remember the fusilli."

I hung my head in despair, wishing he would give us some real advice. What was our plan to break down their defense? Stop Theo and the other winger from crossing the ball so much? And how in the world do you play against midfielders who never get tired and fullbacks who can score from thirty yards out?

But Coach Beppe never got more specific, and I wondered if he was even watching the game. Oh, how I wished Samantha was here.

During the halftime break, I overheard Logan giving Caden words of encouragement. The entire half, Caden had seemed out of sorts and not in the game. He was always a cautious player, but he hadn't even tried to take anyone on or move the ball forward.

On our way back to the field, when the coaches were out of earshot, Aron chastised Caden for not getting him the ball enough. That did not help his confidence. Noticing how down everyone seemed, I called for a huddle. "We're only two goals down," I said. "Plenty of teams come back from that. Remember the last game of the season? Now come on!"

"Yank's right," Brock said. "Buckle up!"

When the second half began, we pressed them hard, and the momentum began to swing. Maybe the Bayonets thought they had already won the game.

Fine. The Dragons had thought the same thing, right before we came back and spoiled their perfect season.

On the Bayonets' next trip downfield, Theo dribbled around Brock and reared back for a shot, only to find himself flat on his back after Riley slide tackled him from behind.

The referee waved his arms. Fair play.

Eddy gathered the loose ball, evaded an attacker, and fed a pass to Otto. To confuse the defense, John had run all the way back to midfield. Otto passed to him, and John flicked the ball to me. A Bayonet player pressed me hard from behind. I feinted one way, turned the other, and sent a line drive pass to Patrick with the outside of my foot, splitting two defenders.

Patrick had to cut inside to receive the ball. I followed my own pass to support him.

"Keeyiiaa!" Patrick yelled as he took a hard shot from the edge of the penalty box.

At the last second, their fullback jumped in front of Patrick to block the shot—but it ricocheted ten yards back to me.

Gaston, their giant center back, was closing in. I thought about taking him on, but then I saw a better opportunity. Aron was making a run towards the far post. If I hit the ball soon, before he passed the defense, he would stay onside.

As Gaston stepped towards me, I struck the ball as if aiming for goal, but instead curved a pass around him towards the back post.

It was on target. Aron bounded high in the air, above the French defender, and snapped a pinpoint header into the goal, just inside the near post.

2–1!

Oh, how we celebrated that goal. We had just scored

against the top team in the tournament and were only one goal behind. When the game restarted, we pressed harder than ever, believing we could win.

But the Bayonets withstood the attack. We almost scored two more times—John hit the post, and Patrick sent a shot just over the crossbar. Either goal might have changed the game. But not long after that, Theo broke free again and nutmegged JoJo for a spectacular goal.

We tried hard over the next twenty minutes, we really did. But they just kept coming. Wave after wave of tall, fast, highly skilled players. They made substitutions who were just as good as the starters. Their attack never seemed to end. The 4–2–3–1 formation is great for keeping possession if you have good midfielders, and they had excellent ones who made triangles all over the field. Otto, Caden and I could not keep up. We were overwhelmed, feeling as if they had two extra players.

The Bayonets scored again, this time on a free kick by Javier.

And again.

And again.

The second half had started so well, especially after our goal, but by the end of the game, the score was 5–1. An embarrassing, lopsided loss. When the final whistle blew, we trudged off the field. What hurt most of all was the feeling they were simply better than us.

In the locker room, Aron ripped off the white practice jersey and threw his arms in the air. "Why didn't you get me the ball more? I could have scored another three goals!"

"Last time I saw you with the ball," Brock said with a growl, "one of their players flattened you."

Aron waved a hand. "That was a lucky tackle. He couldn't handle me."

Wow, I thought. *The only thing in Paris bigger than the Eiffel Tower is this guy's ego.*

"And *you*," Aron continued, turning to face Caden. "Are you out of shape? Didn't you get enough sleep? You were tired out there. You never advanced the ball. You can't just play it back every time."

"That's enough," Coach Beppe said quietly. "Do you see the bees turning on each other in the flowers? Never."

With a sneer, Aron turned his back to the team and began taking off his cleats. The Caden I knew would have lashed out in defense, but instead he put his hands on his knees and lowered his head.

"Why don't you shut up?" Logan said to Aron.

"Boys," Coach Beppe said, more sternly.

"I didn't sign up to play in the second division," Aron said in a huff, slipping on a shirt and his tennis shoes and slinging his bag over his shoulder. "If we can't do any better than this, I'll go to a different team."

ENTRY #8

Missing Jerseys, Messi Magic, and the Mona Lisa

"Maybe Aron *should* go to a different team," Brock said later that day, when the team had gathered for dinner at a pizzeria by the canal. "Like on a deserted island or the moon."

John, Eddy, Otto, and Patrick were sitting with us. We had a table on the patio, with a great view of the water. As usual, Aron was by himself, perched in a lonely corner of the pizzeria, his back to the rest of the team. On the opposite side of the patio, Coach Beppe plunged his fork into a plateful of pasta and twirled it, as happy as a little kid at Halloween with a bag full of candy.

"Good idea, bruv," John said. "Send him to Space Rock F.C."

"His goal rate is quite efficient," Otto added. "I hate to say it, but he is an excellent player."

Patrick put one slice of cheese pizza on top of another and ate them both at the same time. Only he would think of that. "So what? Dude's got issues. He acted like the goal today was all him. Leo did the hard work."

I shook my head. "You and Otto did too. Everyone played well. They were just really, really good."

"We can beat them, though," Eddy said, tapping his fingers on the table to the tune of some invisible beat. "Right?"

The question seemed to hang in the air and make everyone uncomfortable.

"Of course we can," I said finally, after a few bites of pizza. "No one's unbeatable, like we said." I flicked my eyes towards Aron's table. "But we could use him."

Brock snorted. "Not if he's gonna be a jerk."

JoJo walked over to our table, pulled up a chair facing backwards, sat, and jerked her head in Aron's direction. "You gotta be talking about Mr. Perfect."

"How'd you guess?" Brock said. "The big fat L on his head?"

I didn't like the turn the conversation had taken. Aron *was* being a jerk, but he was our teammate, and I worried what would happen if he lashed out at JoJo, Brock, or Riley. That could end up in a fight that got them kicked off the team.

In the locker room after the game, Coach Beppe had criticized Aron's negative behavior and congratulated the team on playing hard and staying with the Bayonets for so long. But as usual, he hadn't offered much direct advice.

Was this how it worked in the pros? Were the players so advanced they didn't need the same kind of coaching? Was it all bees and pasta and juggling lessons atop stone walls that offered no real solutions to our problems?

"What about our jerseys?" I said, to steer the conversation away from Aron. "What do you think happened to them?"

"It's strange, yeah?" John said. "They still haven't turned up. They're not worth anything, so why steal them?"

Brock burped. "It was probably one of the Frenchies. Trying to sabotage us."

"But they gave us the practice jerseys," Eddy said.

"Their *coaches* did. Not the players."

That didn't ring true to me. Paris Saint-Martin didn't need to cheat to win. In fact, it hadn't even crossed my mind that someone wanted us to forfeit the game. I assumed the jerseys had been misplaced or stolen by a hotel employee.

"Maybe they were lost in the laundry," I said weakly, knowing that didn't make sense. I had put my jersey in my duffel bag on my way to breakfast.

Patrick waved a hand. "I bet someone on the street took them. I saw a sketchy dude hanging outside the hotel. He probably waited until the receptionist went to the bathroom, came in, and stole them."

"But why?" Otto said. "John is right. They have very little value."

"I dunno. Maybe he thought they were pro jerseys. Those would be worth something."

That guess seemed as unlikely as the rest. Unsure what to think, we looked at one another uneasily around the table as a boat passed through the canal, its wake causing the murky green water to lap against the shore.

⚽ ⚽ ⚽

After dinner, when we returned to the hotel, the receptionist informed Coach Beppe that our jerseys had been found in a storage closet in the basement. No one had any idea how they had gotten there. The man on duty in the morning *did* remember people hanging out around our bags during breakfast. But they were all our age and coming from the restaurant, so he assumed they were players.

When Coach Beppe questioned us about this, John admitted to searching his bag during breakfast for his headphones.

Otto had retrieved a book to read, Sami had put up his phone, and I had gone to the restroom. Most of the players had returned to the lobby for some reason or another. And, just like me, I assumed everyone kept their game jersey at the top of their bags. It would have been easy to unzip the bags and pluck the jerseys right out of them.

The team's morale was as low as I could remember. Coach Beppe, perhaps to lift our spirits, announced a surprise outing for the evening: a night boat ride down the Seine.

This sounded exciting. As darkness fell over the city, our troubles forgotten for the moment, we took the Metro to Alma-Marceau and walked to a bridge on the river Seine. After descending a set of steps to the bank of the river, we hopped on a double-decker boat with orange seats. During the ride, most of us sat on the large, open deck on top of the boat, enjoying the cool breeze, dangling our legs through the railing, and waving at tourists on the shore. The moon was full and golden, the city lit with millions of lights. We talked and laughed, ignored the boring tour guide on the loudspeaker as we gazed at the impressive landmarks illuminated alongside the river, palaces and cathedrals and museums and, of course, the Eiffel Tower. Passing right by that golden spire at night, soaring high into the sky as if reaching for the stars, was an experience I'll never forget. It inspired me so much that I decided to start writing in my journal again.

On the way home, we stopped for ice cream along the canal and took our time walking back to the hotel. The streets were full of life, and I didn't want the night to end.

⚽ ⚽ ⚽

In the morning, Coach Beppe announced we had the day off. Our next game was three days away, and he wanted us to rest. Instead, he scheduled another sightseeing trip, starting with a destination that had everyone buzzing over breakfast: a tour of the Paris Saint-Germain stadium, the team known to the world as PSG.

You know them, right? The team that once had Messi, Neymar, and Mbappé all at the same time?

How did they ever lose?

PSG plays in a neighborhood on the west side of Paris, a few Metro stops past the Eiffel Tower. We started at the top of the stadium, so we could get a bird's eye view of how big it was. It holds almost fifty thousand people—that's twice the size of my hometown!

After sitting in the VIP boxes and marveling at how nice they were, we toured the locker rooms with blue leather seats and framed jerseys hanging on the walls. It wasn't all about Messi, Neymar, and Mbappé either. All kinds of top players have starred for PSG. It's the most successful club in France, which has won the World Cup twice. That's more than every country except Brazil, Germany, Argentina, and Italy.

When we left the locker rooms, we ran through the tunnel and out to the field just like the players do. I was awestruck by the perfect pitch and the endless rows of bleachers.

On our way out, I saw a ball signed by Messi on display and stopped to stare at it, starstruck. I had never seen anything of Messi's in person. Even his signature impressed me, as if a little piece of him was in the room with us. I remembered Carlos's request for swag, asked John to take a photo of me by the ball, and chuckled to myself. That was the closest Carlos would get to something signed by Messi.

After the tour, we spent the afternoon at the Louvre, the biggest art museum in the world. Even I had to admit the entrance, a glass pyramid surrounded by a gigantic former palace, was impressive.

This is a story about soccer, so I won't bore you with all the details of the art museum. I did like some of the paintings, and the Louvre has a real mummy, though it wasn't as spooky as the one in the British Museum. It also has a painting called the *Mona Lisa*, which is apparently the most famous painting in the world, though I have no idea why. It's just a woman wearing clothes from five hundred years ago sitting in a chair or something. It's hard to even tell what she's doing. I mean, really? The most famous painting in the world?

For some reason, Riley of all people couldn't seem to stop looking at it, though when Brock and JoJo teased him, Riley grew angry and claimed the painting was rubbish and he was just leaning against the wall because he was tired.

Otto, of course, knew all about the different types of paintings and statues. It was like walking around with a teacher or an encyclopedia. John seemed interested as well, probably because he was from London and more sophisticated than the rest of us. Sami's dad probably owned the whole museum, and Patrick spent the afternoon pretending to be a tour guide and inventing hilarious facts about the exhibits. For example, he claimed the *Mona Lisa* had just farted and that's why she looked so pleased with herself. Even Coach Beppe laughed at that one.

At the end of the day, we had a late dinner at the hotel and returned to our rooms. I chatted with John and Eddy for a while, listened to some music, and tried to get some sleep. In the morning, we would leave for Prague, less than two hours away by plane. After that, we only had one full day in the Czech Republic before our game against Prague FC.

A game that, if we wanted to stay alive in the Tournament of Champions, we badly needed to win.

ENTRY #9

Bowties and Castles and Dungeons, Oh My!

We landed in Prague, the capital of the Czech Republic, at noon the next day. I knew it was expensive to fly, but I remembered what Tig had once told me, that if the Knights or the Dragons or any pro team develops just one of their academy players into a star, then the cost of all that training and equipment and travel will be more than worth it.

The Prague U14 team had lost to Perseus Amsterdam, the other team in our group, 2–1. Just like in the Premier League and the World Cup, a win was worth three points in the group stage of the Tournament of Champions. Ties earned one point, and a loss got a big fat zero.

We played each team in the group one time. After the loss to Paris Saint-Martin, the pressure was on to win points against a Prague team who, according to Otto, was ranked 24th in Europe. Except for the ranking, Otto knew very little about our next opponents, other than their reputation for long balls and corner kicks. He said they had very big players—as big as Paris Saint-Martin, maybe even bigger—who loved to play rough and counterattack.

Oh boy, I thought. *That sounds challenging.*

All of a sudden, I pictured Messi rolling his beady lizard eyes, and heard Carlos's voice in my head: *What did you think it would be, doofus? An easy game? It's the Tournament of Champions.*

We took a bus from the airport to our hotel in the suburbs. When I say *suburbs*, I don't mean suburbs like America has, with lots of space and big cars and houses. Our hotel was located in an area full of large stone buildings with fresh paint. People lived in apartments on the upper stories, and there were shops and restaurants at the bottom. Just like in France and England, all the buildings were close together and I didn't see a single green lawn.

During lunch, Coach Beppe gave us the schedule for our visit. This afternoon, we had a three-hour practice, followed by a trip to the historic center of Prague. In the morning, we were taking a short trip to a village with a castle, combined with another special soccer practice that Coach Beppe wouldn't discuss. Our game was on the third day. That same evening, we would take an overnight train to Amsterdam.

⚽   ⚽   ⚽

The afternoon practice took place on a soccer field in a park just three blocks from our hotel. The field had been reserved and there was even a sign welcoming our team to the city. As we began to warm up, a crowd of people gathered to watch, mostly teens and younger kids. They oohed and aahed as we juggled, passed, and took long-range shots on goal. It felt good to have admirers and gave a little extra energy to my warmups.

"Who plays for the Czech Republic, anyway?" Brock said as we waited in line to practice penalties. "Anybody good?"

Otto leaned over to stretch a hamstring. "Surely you've heard of Nevded, Rosicky, Jan Koller?"

"Nope."

"Me either," I said.

Otto put a hand to his forehead. "Those are legendary players. Okay, then—what about Peter Cech?"

"Duh," Brock and I said at the same time.

"Yo, he was a Gunner," John added, right before he took a penalty shot that JoJo dove at and swatted away.

Caden snorted. "Yeah, but his best years were at Chelsea, not Arsenal."

"Many people," Otto said, "me included, consider Peter Cech the greatest Premier League goalie of all time."

That impressed me, and I wondered how good the Prague U14 goalie would be.

"Okay, everyone," Coach Beppe said after two more rounds of penalty kicks. "Bring it in."

We gathered in front of him and took a knee on the thick grass. The day was warm and humid, the birds chirping and the insects buzzing, the smell of pine on the breeze. We could have been in a park in Ohio except for the local kids shouting in Czech on a playground near the field. Oh, and a cart rolling by with an advertisement for a strange dessert that resembled an ice cream dumpling crossed with a hot dog.

I wiped a bead of sweat off my forehead and waited, once again, for our coach to teach us a fancy new move or a world-class trick on defense. When everyone had quieted down, Coach Beppe stuck out a hand and opened it, walking slowly along the line of players so everyone could see what he was holding.

It was not another fusilli, I was happy to see.

But it was a different kind of pasta.

"Behold the farfalle," Coach Beppe said in a somber voice, as if showing off a diamond ring instead of a piece of dried dough. "Also known as the bowtie pasta, because of its particular shape. Do you see?"

He pinched it between two fingers, held it up, and turned it slowly back and forth. I squinted in the sun and agreed that it resembled a pasta version of one of the bowties my Uncle Jerry—my mom's brother—liked to wear.

"We have four points at the end, *sí*? And a tiny little point in the middle. We have all heard of triangle passing, I am sure. You have probably practiced this all your lives."

There was a murmur of agreement, though I stayed quiet, because I had only learned about the magic of triangle passing at the academy summer camp.

"A very effective tool," he continued, "which I prefer to call pizza passing. But what, I ask of you, is an even better option under pressure than having two passing targets?"

Patrick raised a hand. "Eating a lot of pasta?"

Some of us chuckled, but Coach Beppe pressed on. "The four ends of the bowtie. A square. An attacker with three passing options instead of two. We will practice this today, though we will not make it so simple as four against one defender or even two. You must learn to *shape* your pasta during the game, under high pressure, at a moment's notice."

I understood his point, but I still had to work not to giggle, because I just couldn't get the image of an Italian chef out of my mind, making the dough in his hands and slinging perfectly formed bowties across the field during a game.

Now, you might not believe an entire soccer practice can be built around yet another kind of pasta, but I assure you, Coach Beppe is a genius at making drills out of Italian food.

Remember the simple passing drill with four cones arranged in a square, three passers, and a defender in the middle? Where the players without the ball have to run to the open cones every time and form triangles? We did a similar drill in a much larger space with twelve cones, six passers, and four defenders. It was tricky to understand, but Coach Beppe showed us how to move around and form squares on different cones, trying to outwit the defenders. He walked around to guide us, waving his hands and shouting "Make the bowtie!" Eventually we moved on to small-sided scrimmages, where instead of scoring we had to complete passes to each of the twelve cones before a defender stole the ball.

We worked on bowtie passing for two whole hours. By the time we finished practice, I was exhausted and a little confused and absolutely sick of hearing about pasta.

⚽ ⚽ ⚽

Later that evening, after we had returned to the hotel and showered, we took a trip to the Prague Old Town, which is called Staré Město. Don't ask me how to pronounce that because I have no idea. I thought French was a strange language until I arrived in Prague and heard the Czech people speak. Not only does it sound even more foreign, but the Czech language has a completely different alphabet, called Cyrillic. The signs on the roads and buildings are a jumble of shapes and symbols. It's frustrating—but only because I wish I could read all the signs and understand what everyone was saying. Maybe one day, if I get to play professional soccer in Europe, I can learn some foreign languages.

On our way out, I was excited to learn that Prague has a

Metro. We didn't take it that evening because the bus route was closer to our destination. Half an hour after leaving the hotel, we hopped off the bus and walked another few minutes into the heart of Prague.

To be honest, I wasn't expecting that much. I had already seen London and Paris. How amazing could another big city be? Especially one I had barely heard of?

Let me tell you how wrong I was.

Not only is Prague completely different from London and Paris, it's also incredible. Unbelievable, even, if I hadn't seen it with my own eyes. I've already told you I don't care that much about buildings and architecture and all that. Which is true. But the entire Old Town of Prague was like walking through a real-life fairy tale city. Not the childish kind of fairy tale you might be thinking about, but something more like *Harry Potter* or *Lord of the Rings* or an awesome anime. I'm talking spooky cobblestone streets and foggy bridges with ancient statues and black towers and huge authentic castles right in the middle of the town.

London and Paris have plenty of old buildings, but they're scattered around. In the center of Prague, *everything* looks a thousand years old. If a bunch of knights rode by in full armor on horseback I wouldn't have been surprised. London and Paris feel modern in comparison.

After showing us around, Coach Beppe announced it was time for dinner. To our shock, he guided us down a set of stone steps that led underground. At the bottom, we passed through an archway into a room carved straight out of the rock. I was even more stunned to find waiters, guests, and wooden candlelit tables filling the room. It felt more like a dungeon than a restaurant, except there were no skeletons hanging from chains on the walls (that was disappointing). In fact, the name of the place was The Dungeon.

To my great relief—we had eaten a lot of unfamiliar food over the last few days—this bizarre place had a menu in English and a cheeseburger with fries. I sat with my friends at the creepiest table we could find, deep in one of the cobwebbed corners, and wondered who had built this place so long ago, and why.

On the way back to the hotel, I decided I liked Prague just as much, if not more, than the other places I had seen.

It had been a long day. Otto and I were sharing a double room this time, and we both crashed as soon as we arrived. In the morning, over breakfast, Coach Beppe announced it was time for another surprise practice.

ENTRY #10

The Amazing Race

After breakfast, we took a train from Prague that followed a river for part of the journey. The ride took less than an hour, and we saw little towns and villages along the way.

So far, all we knew was that we were visiting a famous castle outside Prague. What did that have to do with soccer? Did Coach Beppe plan for us to juggle on a wall again? Maybe on top of the castle, with a long drop into the moat if we fell?

Our train pulled to a stop alongside a different river surrounded by shaggy green hills and fields with bales of hay. We exited along with a bunch of other tourists, then crossed a footbridge over the river that led to a village at the bottom of a hill. I looked up and saw, past the village and a patch of forest, a castle perched at the very top of the hill. It looked as I had always imagined a castle would, with towers and peaked roofs and a high wall to keep out invaders.

"Shall we visit this lovely castle?" Coach Beppe asked. "The walk is one and a half miles. I urge you," he said with a knowing smile, "to pay attention to your surroundings along the way. It is good to know where you are at all times, who is around you and what routes you can take, both on the pitch and in life."

None of us knew what he was talking about, and there was still no mention of a practice. And by the time we had walked up the long steep road through the village and toured the castle, then headed back down to leave, Coach Beppe *still* hadn't mentioned a word about a ball or a game.

With a shrug, wondering if he had forgotten, I strolled down the hill with my friends, glancing at the tourist shops and restaurants lining the road but not seeing much of interest except for a boba shop. Coach Beppe let us stop there for a treat. Vehicles were not allowed on the main road, so we didn't have to worry about cars and could walk without paying attention to our surroundings, ignoring Coach Beppe's odd request.

At the bottom of the hill, right at the entrance to the village, he gathered everyone together and clapped his hands. "Now," he said, "are we ready to begin?"

One of our managers walked over lugging a huge bag over his shoulder. He opened it and started passing out soccer balls as we looked on in confusion.

Riley put a foot on his ball to stop it from rolling away. "Uh, ur, ready for wut?"

"For the race." Coach Beppe pointed to the top of the hill. "To the castle and back. The winner will receive a prize I think you will appreciate."

We all stared dumbfounded at the long winding road stuffed with locals and tourists of all ages, dogs on leashes, bicycles, scooters, and baby strollers. It would be hard to navigate through that crowd with any speed.

On the left side of the road, a shallow stream flowed through a stone canal. Every now and then, a footbridge spanned the stream, leading to shops and side roads and houses.

"Do you mean we're racing with our balls?" I asked.

"But of course. You are footballers, are you not? You may

reach the castle using any route you wish and using any body part except your hands. A manager is waiting in the courtyard of the castle to mark the halfway point."

Brock threw up his hands. "But what are the rules?"

"The rules? You may walk or run, hide or crawl, steal or kick another player's ball, sprint along the rooftops or swim in the stream. No, actually, do not do either of those things. But in general, you may proceed how you wish. Please be careful and do not injure yourself or anyone else. Those are the only guidelines. I hope you were paying attention on our walk, as I suggested. Now," he said, glancing at his watch and flinging his hands forward, "go!"

Caught off guard by the unexpected challenge and the sudden command, I surged forward, pushing my ball down the cobblestone sidewalk on the right side of the road, which had fewer people and bikes and scooters. Almost at once the ball hit the edge of a large stone and bounced to the side. I saw others having the same problem. The sidewalk was tough to dribble on. The main road was paved and much wider but had more obstacles. All the pedestrians seemed to prefer walking up the middle of the traffic-free road.

A choice, then: dribble down the cobblestone sidewalk, or weave in and out of people on the road?

I had a better idea.

"Well done, Leo!" Coach Beppe shouted as I lifted the ball in the air, caught it between my shoulder blades, and began to run up the road. "Very creative!"

Maybe it was creative, but I wasn't sure how smart it was. Both John and Aron pulled ahead, able to dribble faster on the cobblestones than I could run uphill with a ball pinched between my shoulders. When I swerved to avoid a child running in my path, I dropped the ball and knew I had to switch tactics.

What was everyone else doing? I turned and saw a variety of strategies.

Sami was in the middle of the road, doing his best to weave in and out of people on the street. He was slow but an excellent dribbler, so that was a good choice. Brock was charging up the sidewalk, roaring at people to move and pushing his ball along the cobblestones with brute force.

Patrick had jumped the stream and headed into the forested hillside, trying to find a more direct route to the castle through the woods. Maybe he would get lucky and find a trail. More likely, he would get lost and need help.

Caden and Logan were working together, passing one ball between them. I supposed they planned to split the prize if they won. Coach Beppe gave no sign this was not allowed, and so far, their strategy was working. They had taken the lead, moving ahead of John and Aron.

At the rear of the pack, JoJo struggled to move through the crowd. She was a goalie and did not have the best foot skills. I felt bad for her, but Coach Beppe had said no hands.

Eddy was making steady progress, moving his hips and bobbing his head, dancing as he dribbled on the road.

Where were Riley and Otto? At first I didn't see either of them, but then I caught a glimpse of Otto crossing a bridge over the stream and veering up an alley. If anyone had paid attention to the route on our walk and knew the best way to win, it was Otto.

And then I saw what Riley was doing: running around trying to sabotage the other players. He snuck up behind Sami and poked his ball away, causing it to roll downhill to Coach Beppe. As Sami gave chase on his stubby legs, Riley turned and sprinted towards Eddy. At the last second, Eddy saw him and tried to dribble away, but Riley kicked his ball off the street and into the stream.

Ouch. Eddy flung up a hand in frustration and ran after it.

Where was Riley's ball? Guessing he had hidden it and would double back later, I veered to the left and followed Otto down the alley, deciding to leverage his big brain and stay away from Riley.

"Wise decision, Leo," Otto said when he heard me dribbling and glanced over his shoulder. The alley was paved and free of people, making it easy to move.

"I figured you were paying attention."

I regretted the compliment when, three blocks later, the alley curved to the right and dead-ended at a brick wall. With a sinking feeling, I started to turn back when I saw Otto slip through the wall and disappear.

What?

I raced closer and saw a sliver of space between the buildings. I followed my Hungarian friend through the little walkway, jumping over a pile of broken glass before re-emerging on the main road. I looked down the hill and realized we were in the lead, almost a block ahead of John and Aron.

Otto continued down the sidewalk. I hesitated and moved into the road, joining the crush of tourists moving up the paved surface towards the castle looming in the distance. For a while, I wove through people and pets and lampposts, trying to keep an eye on my teammates at the same time. Whenever

I glanced back, I saw Riley trying to steal someone's ball, and wondered how he managed to make any progress. Was he planning to kick everyone's ball deep into the forest, then finish on his own?

Good luck, I thought grimly. *You're not getting my ball.*

Shops and restaurants passed by in a blur.

A pig on a leash caused me to cut hard to the right and dribble around both the pig and its owner.

Wait—a pig?

I blinked and kept going.

The road turned sharply to the left, followed by a grueling spell of uphill dribbling. Outside a skateboard shop, a group of teenagers with Mohawks and heavy metal T-shirts jeered at me and waved their arms, trying to break my concentration. I focused on my ball and ignored them.

About a mile into the race, the town faded away as the paved road narrowed to a footpath that led through the forest and up to the castle. This was the final portion of the route. Not as many tourists, but there was a stone wall on my left and a drop-off down the hill on my right. The slope of the hill was not dangerous, but if I lost my ball, it would roll forever.

I was still in the lead, but when I peered over my shoulder, I saw Aron and John and Otto close behind, chugging steadily forward.

At last, I reached the top. The footpath opened up as I raced into the courtyard of the castle, working hard to control my ball on the cobblestones, exhausted by the hard run uphill. I saw the team manager near the ticket stand, waving to signal the halfway point. I thought I had reached him first when, incredibly, a ball bounced into the courtyard out of nowhere, and I saw Patrick climb over a stone wall with a big grin on his face. That maniac must have hiked all the way through the woods with his ball!

But Patrick didn't reach the checkpoint first. As I watched in shock, Caden sprinted past me without a ball, raced across the courtyard, stole Patrick's ball, and kicked it back into the forest.

Chaos erupted. Patrick roared and started to run after Caden, then realized Caden didn't have a ball. Instead, Patrick turned and cornered Logan, who shielded him off and passed to Caden. The two of them played keep-away as Patrick chased them around.

I fist-bumped the manager, turned, and began racing down the hill for the return journey. Aron and John stayed right with me, but Otto didn't have as much stamina and started to fall behind.

On the way down, I passed some of the second-team players, JoJo, and then Brock on the footpath through the woods. JoJo was hunched over, concentrating on her ball, while Brock growled and said, "Out of my way, Leo."

I was happy to obey, knowing he would never catch me. Just in case, I protected my ball as I passed him, then ran into Eddy. We slapped hands, knowing we would never hurt each other's chances. I also passed Sami, then re-entered the town as the pathway merged into the road.

A short way later, when I made that sharp turn to the right, I caught a blur of movement in the corner of my eye. On instinct, I threw my body in front of my ball just as Riley jumped out from behind a trash can. Knowing how tough he was, I bent down and leaned my weight back, keeping him at bay with my arms in shielding position. He pressed hard against my back to get my ball, reaching through my legs and then trying to run around me. I held him off, but it came at a price: Aron sped past me, gaining the lead.

Realizing I wasn't an easy target, Riley switched course and moved to confront John as he came down the hill.

I was off again.

As I streaked away, I saw Riley and John locked in a tough battle and knew the delay would cost them. I focused on my own path, dodging in and out of tourists like a race car driver. Of course, they were all laughing and pointing at us, wondering what in the world we were doing. Some of the younger kids tried to get us to pass the ball to them.

I glanced back again. No one else was close except Aron, who was half a block ahead of me, his thick legs and blond flat top bobbing through the crowd.

The town sped by. It was lunchtime, so the road was not as busy and the patio tables outside the restaurants had filled with people. Going downhill was much easier on my legs but made it harder to control the ball. I was forced to slow down, because if I did lose the ball, it could roll into the stream or all the way to the bottom of the hill. I doubted Coach Beppe would allow someone to finish without control of their ball.

Up ahead, three small children ran straight into Aron's path, causing him to stop in frustration as the parents hurried over to gather their kids.

"Tough luck," I said as I sped by him. Startled I was so close, he lashed out with a foot to steal my ball, but I danced away and kept going.

Now I could see the start of the village, less than a soccer field away. Coach Beppe waved his arms, urging me on.

I smiled in satisfaction, knowing it was too late for anyone to catch me and that I had won—right before I looked back a final time and saw JoJo racing down the road on a skateboard like a champion snow skier on a downhill slalom. She was sitting down on the board and somehow, incredibly, bringing the ball alongside her with her foot, kicking it forward every few feet.

Right behind her were the group of teenagers I had seen outside of the comic and manga shop. They were also on skateboards and cheering for JoJo who, with her purple hair and silver nose stud and pasty white skin, fit right in with their punk rock look.

I tried to speed up but knew there was no way I could outrun her. JoJo was moving too fast. I had to switch my strategy. There was only one way to stop her, and I would only have one chance to do it.

I left my ball and let it keep rolling, hoping I could catch up to it before it reached Coach Beppe. Then I raced across the street to confront JoJo as she flew by on her skateboard. As I stabbed at her ball, she flicked it over my foot with a deft maneuver, veered to the side with a power slide, then shot forward again and regained possession of her ball.

"Didn't I tell you?" she taunted as she flew downhill. "I'm even better at skating than blocking shots."

Nope, I thought as I stood in the middle of the road with my hands on my hips, watching JoJo reach the bottom of the road, slap hands with Coach Beppe, and throw her arms into the air in victory.

She definitely forgot to mention that.

ENTRY #11

Prague FC

"Well done, everyone," Coach Beppe said when we gathered at the bottom of the hill where the race had started.

Surprisingly, no one had lost their ball, though Patrick came in last, finishing long after everyone else and arriving through the woods with a sheepish expression. Riley, as I had suspected, retrieved his ball from behind a trash can near the start of the race. He had a satisfied smirk on his face as if, all along, he had cared more about sabotaging the other players than winning.

"Let's all give JoJo a hand," our coach continued. "I did not expect such an unusual finish, but she did use her feet, and I did not prohibit skateboards, so JoJo is our winner!"

We gave her a round of applause, then booed and called her a cheater. It was all done in a joking manner, except for Aron, who seemed genuinely upset that Coach Beppe had allowed JoJo to win on a skateboard.

"What's the matter?" I said, deciding to roast him a little. "You would have come in second to me anyway."

Aron snarled and turned his back.

As for JoJo, she shook a fist in the air, seeming to enjoy being the villain. Her new friends wandered off after JoJo returned the skateboard.

"What did we learn today?" Coach Beppe asked. "The

value of stamina, creativity, and observation. Often you must adjust to your circumstances and figure out the best way forward on your own."

"Yo, Coach Bep," JoJo shouted. "What's my prize?"

With a smile, Coach Beppe reached into a backpack at his feet and withdrew a framed photo, holding it against his chest so we could not see the front.

"Hey, Jo," Brock teased, "you won some art for all your trouble. You love art, right?"

We all knew how bored she had been—or claimed to have been—at the Louvre.

"It's probably the *Mona Lisa*," John added. "Your favorite."

"Nah," Riley chimed in. "It's a bunch of old blokes sitting around staring at their belly buttons."

We all laughed, and I was surprised that Riley had spoken so many words at one time.

"What's this?" JoJo said as Coach Beppe turned the photo around, revealing a soccer team posing in a huddle. A player in the middle was holding a trophy. The white jerseys had yellow and blue trim, and I recognized them at once as belonging to Real Madrid, Barcelona's archrival and one of the best teams in the world. Handwritten signatures covered the edges of the photo.

"Wait," Brock said. "Is that *Real Madrid*? And all the players' *signatures*?"

Coach Beppe handed the photo to JoJo. "Indeed."

"Wait—she gets to keep it?" John said. "Whoa, JoJo, you scored. It's a copy, though, right?"

"Oh no. Those are actual signatures. I was the assistant coach that year, and we had just won the Champions League."

John's jaw slowly dropped, as did mine. As I took a better look at the photo, I realized the faces belonged to some of the most famous players in the world.

This wasn't a random piece of swag. It was a priceless gift.

"You're giving this away?" I asked, incredulous he would part ways with something like that just for winning a silly race.

"I have many mementos. Why should they collect dust on my shelf? I believe in inspiring the next generation."

None of us were laughing at JoJo now. Instead we crowded around her, jealous and awestruck as she held the signed photo in her hands, careful not to smudge the glass.

⚽ ⚽ ⚽

We had a late lunch in the village and returned to Prague. Coach Beppe let us walk around Old Town again, and we found whole new sections to explore. After dinner, we returned to the hotel to relax and prepare for the game, which started at noon the next day.

Despite our opening loss to Paris Saint-Martin, our spirits were high, and I couldn't wait to get on the field.

⚽ ⚽ ⚽

The Prague FC U14 stadium was the smallest one we had played at in some time. Their academy was a short bus ride from our hotel, inside a sprawling park on a hill with a view of Prague's red roofs and medieval spires.

As we warmed up, I saw what Otto had meant. Their players were enormous. I assumed they were fourteen going on fifteen, about to switch age groups next season, but if someone had told me they were all sixteen, I would have believed them. Their goalie had a moustache.

"Bah," Coach Beppe said in the huddle before the game. "Do not worry about their size. You will run around them, *sí*, like cheetahs around a buffalo. You will use your fusilli and your bowties and leave them grasping at your jerseys."

Otto raised a hand. "Which tactic should we use, Coach? Triangle passing or squares?"

He shrugged. "Whichever you need. Now!" he said as he clapped his hands. "Good luck, and do not disappoint yourselves."

Why would we disappoint ourselves? I thought as we ran out.

And do cheetahs really run circles around buffalos? They might be faster, but buffalos are far bigger and probably chase the cheetahs away.

Thanks again, Coach.

I quickly noticed that Prague FC used a 4–3–3, the same formation we did. Their center midfielder, my main opponent for the day, was also their number 10. He had long blond hair tied in a ponytail, tree trunks for legs, and bright orange cleats. As the whistle blew, he received a pass and ran straight at me with the ball. He towered over me and might have been the biggest player on their team. I gritted my teeth and stepped up to challenge him. He made a nifty pass at the last moment, showing a nice bit of skill just before we collided.

And when I say we *collided*, I mean I bounced off his Godzilla-like frame and fell to the ground, while he barely flinched and kept running.

Oh boy, I thought as I leaped to my feet and brushed off the grass. *This is gonna be a rough day.*

The same guy—his jersey read Krek, which made me think

of Shrek and reinforced my belief he was some sort of ogre instead of a human—received the ball again near the edge of the penalty box. I could already tell he was the engine of their team.

Brock stepped up to challenge him. After Krek passed to a teammate, Brock gave him a little shove in retaliation for flattening me. The referee snapped a warning but did not call a foul.

Krek didn't seem to notice. He curled to the side and received another pass. By this time, I had raced back, and I stripped the ball out from under him. With a grunt, he turned and tried a slide tackle, but I skipped away and lifted a pass to Caden across the field.

The midfielder on Caden's side was almost as enormous as Krek. My pass was a little short, and the two of them reached the ball at the same time. Caden tried to shield his defender, which he was good at, but the Prague midfielder plowed over him, collected the ball, and sent it down the line.

The ref waved his arms. Still no foul.

The Prague winger streaked down the sideline. I could tell Sami was in trouble. He was undersized *and* a little slow. Sure enough, the winger kicked it forward and raced right past him. The move was nothing special, except for the speed of the player.

Riley slid over to intercept him. The winger passed to Krek. I closed him down, cutting off his path to goal. He took a dribble to the right and launched a shot from thirty yards out. It was a good shot, true and hard, but I had forced him into a bad angle, and it was headed right at JoJo. Maybe he just wanted to make sure she was awake.

JoJo stuck out her hands for the routine save, ready to catch the ball and fling it downfield. Krek's long-range shot smacked into her gloves—then slid right off them and squirted into the goal.

For a second, there was silence on the field. Even our opponents were shocked they had scored. JoJo stared at her hands in disbelief and then back at the goal, her shoulders slumped in dejection.

What in the world?

JoJo would never miss an easy save like that. When the ball hit her hands, it had seemed as if her gloves were coated in grease.

As the Prague players began to celebrate, I shouted encouragement to JoJo, not wanting her to get down on herself. But she wasn't listening. Instead, she rubbed her gloves together and frowned. Then she stripped them off, threw them behind the goal in disgust, and sprinted to the sideline while the referee gathered the ball.

"My gloves!" she shouted to one of the managers. "I need my old gloves!"

Before every game, JoJo had a ritual: She kept her fancy game gloves in her bag near the bench and warmed up with a pair of gloves she had used for years. Those things were dinosaurs. One of her uncles had passed them down to her, so the gloves were too big for JoJo's hands. They also had holes in the palms, and the leather was peeling off the fingers. Still, they were her first pair of goalie gloves. She considered them her good luck charm, so she always warmed up with them.

But she couldn't use those worn-out things in a high-level academy game.

Could she?

The referee, annoyed by the delay, blew the whistle for us to kickoff. Unsure what had happened, I put the incident aside and concentrated on the game. We were down 1–0 and had a goalie with a pair of gloves that were two decades old. Why hadn't she asked the backup keeper to lend her a pair?

John kicked off to Patrick, who flicked the ball to Otto. After a few dribbles, Otto sent the ball to me and ran an overlap. Krek didn't give me time to think. As soon as I received the ball, he was on top of me, breathing hard, smothering me with his size. He was fast too. I faked a pass to Otto and pulled back, narrowly avoiding getting flattened again, and managed to squeeze a pass to Eddy.

My Bolivian friend, one of the few players on our team who could match our opponents' size, shouldered off a defender as he ran upfield. Eddy completed a nice give-and-go with Patrick, then took a shot from the edge of the penalty box.

Their keeper saved it with ease. I wondered if he was related to Peter Cech.

"Good hit!" Coach Beppe called out, then bent down to study the grass.

At least we had a shot on goal. We went back and forth with them for a while, but the rest of the half proved the truth of Otto's scouting report. They did not have as much as skill as we did, but they had size and speed and loved to use long balls, counterattacks, and free kicks. I cringed every time they took a corner kick or a direct kick in dangerous territory. Their giant players would crash the box, trying to create havoc as the kick soared in. Brock stood up to them time and again, matching their size and strength, and even Aron started coming back to help, lending his big frame to the defensive effort. Eddy did well, too, and Riley played like a crazed wolverine, sprinting all over the place, sacrificing his wiry body for slide tackles. Riley was not intimidated in the slightest, and the Prague players seemed taken aback by his ferocious play. They started avoiding his side and attacking Eddy and Brock more.

Despite the condition of JoJo's gloves, she held her own, and even made a few key saves to keep us in the game. At halftime, the score was still 1–0. We had only had two shots and desperately needed more offense.

"What happened?" Sami asked JoJo as we gathered around her on the bench.

"What happened?" JoJo repeated, her face twisted in fury. She had carried her game gloves to the huddle. "What happened is someone wrecked my gloves! Feel 'em. They got Vaseline or something on 'em, I dunno."

She passed the gloves around. When I slid my fingers over the palms, the leather surface felt as slick as oil. I looked up in shock. "You're right."

"Course I'm right," she snapped. "Do you think I'd let that soppy shot slip through my fingers?" She threw the gloves on the ground. "Couldn't trust any other pair. Had to go with my own. And I'll stick with 'em too."

I sucked in a breath. This was obviously no accident.

In Paris, I had come to accept that one of the Saint-Martin players, or one of their fans or a parent, had tried to sabotage our team by hiding our jerseys in the basement of the hotel. But now we were hundreds of miles from Paris, in a whole new country. This could only mean one thing.

Someone traveling with us, maybe even one of *our* players, was behind these stunts.

Coach Beppe bent down to study JoJo's gloves. The rest of us, suddenly suspicious of one another, looked warily around the huddle.

"No," Brock said with a growl. "Don't do that. Someone's trying to divide us. Hurt us. Make us lose. When I find out who did this . . ." He made a fist and smacked his own palm. "For now, we have to forget it and move on. We're behind and can't afford another loss in group play."

"He's right," I said. "We have to focus more than ever. If we lose this game, there's no way we advance."

"Yeah, bruvs," John said. "Let's take it to these brutes."

Our coach gave us some advice, none of it helpful, and we retook the field to start the second half. For some reason, an image of my bearded dragon entered my mind as John kicked the ball off to me.

And Messi was not happy.

What are you doing? I could almost hear him saying. *Has size ever mattered to you before? Or to me? I might be tiny, but am I not the king of my jungle? Why are you letting these overgrown clowns boss you around?*

When I looked up, Krek was bearing down on me. I realized I had lost concentration by thinking about Messi, and it was too late to regain it. Krek stripped the ball and shouldered me away so hard I lost my balance and stumbled.

One of their players snickered as he passed me.

They think I'm a pushover.

And right now, I am.

Prague FC made a run down Sami's side, trying to take advantage of him again. But Sami had gotten smarter and backed off the winger, not letting him blow by him, steering him towards the sideline. It cost Sami some ground—the winger kept advancing—but it gave Riley time to swing over and help. As the winger tried to cut inside, Riley flattened him with a slide tackle, dishing out some of their own medicine. Sami recovered the ball and made a quick one-touch pass to Caden.

All game long, and the last game as well, Caden had seemed intimidated by the other team. This was unlike him. For all his faults, Caden had fight. But this summer had been different. He just wasn't himself.

As Caden received the pass, Aron called for the ball, pleading for a long chip. But Caden hesitated and returned the ball to Sami.

Aron threw up his arms. "Come on! Get me the ball!"

Sami made another quick pass, this time a diagonal ball to me. As usual, Krek was all up on me, breathing down my neck, not letting me turn. This time, I didn't fight too hard, letting him think he had me under control.

As the pass came in, I waited until the last moment, then redirected the ball with the bottom of my foot just a fraction—but enough to send it through Krek's thick legs.

I spun around him, pushing off his waist with a hand, leaving him in the dust.

For the first time all game, I had an open field. I pressed forward, dribbling hard, surveying my options.

A defender stepped up. I led Otto with a pass and surged forward. Otto knew exactly what to do. He gave it right back to me, just in front of the defense. Their right center back, a huge redhead with a buzz cut, stepped up to close me down. Pretending to pass to Patrick, who was streaking down the left wing, I stutter-stepped, freezing the defender, then pushed the ball to the right with the outside of my foot and breezed past him.

Their other center back was forced to race over to stop my path to goal. As soon as he did, I curled a ball around him with my right foot. My aim was true, and the ball spun and rolled into the penalty box—right in stride for Aron.

Our Swiss winger took two big steps, met the ball squarely, and stuck it in the top right corner like placing a stamp on an envelope.

The keeper never had a chance.

Tie game!

Aron raced to the sideline and thrust a fist in the air. We all ran over to congratulate him. I thought he might thank me for the perfect pass, but he didn't say a word or even fist bump me.

Over the next portion of the game, we had lots of possession. Our opponents preferred to play on the wings and seemed content to let us control the middle. But every time we pushed forward, they closed us down. As the half went on, we knew we couldn't sit back and pass the ball around. We had to make something happen.

Otto tried to slip a pass to John through two defenders. Their red-headed center back intercepted the ball and kicked it upfield to Krek. I played him tight, forcing him to pass. He was a step faster than I was on a long run, but I had quicker feet, and could defend him and out-dribble him any day of the week.

The Prague right winger sprinted past Eddy and unleashed a big cross from the corner. Brock rose to head the ball away, but an attacker headed it back into the box.

There was a scramble for the ball. Riley tried a slide tackle and missed. Their striker spun around Sami, took another dribble, and blasted a line drive from the penalty spot towards the bottom left corner. I thought for sure it was a goal until JoJo dove, stretched out her entire body, and caught the ball with the fingertips of her worn-out gloves, pushing the shot to the side.

What a save!

"Get back," Brock roared, windmilling his arms to make sure we all helped out on the corner kick.

I let Eddy guard Krek and searched for a smaller player to defend. As the ball curved in, I thought I had my man covered, but he dove around me for a header. The ball screamed towards the far post, where Caden was standing guard. He took the ball in the stomach, stopping the goal, and Riley cleared it out.

"You okay?" I asked Caden. He was bent over double, gasping for breath.

"Fine," he managed to respond. "Go!"

"Great save," I told him, then sprinted upfield.

The Prague defense held firm on our counterattack. We had to retreat. When I received a pass near half field with my back to their goal, Krek pressed me from behind again, so close I could smell his sweat. I used all my strength to shield him off. Before I could find a pass, he ran me over, shoving me to the ground and retrieving the ball.

This time the whistle blew, and the referee awarded me a free kick.

Krek threw up his hands up and said something in Czech. The referee gave him a yellow card for dissent. I smiled to myself because I knew, as strong as Krek was, that I could shield him off and make him foul me.

I took the free kick and lofted it high in the air, trying to reach Patrick. "Luckabucka!" he cried, leaping high over his taller defender to head the ball down the line. He gave chase as I pushed forward with the rest of our offense.

Aron called for another cross, but that hadn't worked all game. The Prague defenders were too tall. After cutting inside, Patrick used the bottom of his foot to roll the ball back to Otto, who was trailing him.

A defender stepped up. Otto let the ball roll through his own legs, fooling the defender. Somehow Otto knew that Eddy was there to continue the play. Eddy took one touch, using his momentum to dribble past a defender, then passed to John in the middle.

Using his powerful squat body, John shielded off a much bigger defender, even managing to turn and surge forward. A center back stepped up. John fed Patrick a slick pass on the goal line. Aron was still waving his arms, desperate for the ball. Patrick pointed his way, shouted, and reared back for a big cross.

Then he fooled everyone by sending the ball backwards again, this time a sharp pass on the ground to the edge of the penalty box—right where I was waiting.

The angle wasn't great, but I took the shot and clanged it off the crossbar. The keeper scrambled to collect the ricochet, but he was a step slower than John, who had snuck inside, followed my shot, and toe-poked it between the keeper's legs.

Goal!

A team effort had led to John's simple toe-poke. Even

Aron had participated by drawing a defender and the attention of the goalkeeper. But as the rest of us celebrated, Aron jogged back upfield, looking angry that he had not been the one to score.

"Great play," John said, slapping me on the back.

"You too," I murmured as I watched Aron turn away, annoyed that he was hurting our team chemistry.

As the second half progressed, our Swiss winger became more and more upset, throwing his hands in the air and badgering Caden to pass him the ball. Finally, Coach Beppe subbed Aron out. He walked off the field in a huff.

The next fifteen minutes were tough. Prague FC made run after run down the sideline, trying to get behind our defense and win corner kicks. But Sami and Eddy stayed strong on the wings, and Brock and Riley patrolled the middle like killer whales circling back and forth in a pool. JoJo made two more excellent saves, each time looking at her gloves in surprise.

I glanced at the digital scoreboard and noticed the time on the game clock time had run out. In its place, a plus sign and another number had appeared.

Three minutes of extra time.

Our opponents grew desperate, and the game got ragged. Everyone was exhausted in mind and body. Players threw themselves to the ground for slide tackles and launched into the air for headers. I felt bruised all over from jostling with Krek for ninety minutes. But as I shielded the ball in midfield again, keeping possession until I found the right pass, the ref finally blew the whistle to signal the end of the game.

We had our first win in the Tournament of Champions.

ENTRY #12

Detectives and Demigods

In the huddle after the game, Aron pointed a finger in Caden's face. "You have to play better. Be more aggressive."

Caden smacked his finger away and shoved him in the chest. "Shut up, ball hog."

As Aron came back at Caden with a raised fist, John grabbed Aron's arm to stop the swing, and Brock grabbed his other arm.

"Easy now, bruv," John said. "Were you paying attention? We just won the game."

Aron shook them off but stepped away from Caden. "We could have won by two more," Aron muttered. "If this team could get me the ball."

"Son," Coach Beppe said in a pained voice, "that is not how we conduct ourselves. Do you see the bees in the hive arguing with each other about who is better or what task to perform?"

Aron looked as if he might retort, thought better of it, and stormed to the bench. He sat at the very edge, took a drink from his water bottle, and glowered at the ground with his hands on his elbows. I knew Samantha would never put up with that behavior, but she wasn't here.

Coach Beppe eyed the rest of us with a grave expression. "Bees that do not work together as one unit cannot survive. It is essential to the proper functioning of the colony."

He continued talking for some time, congratulating us on the hard-fought win, discussing the lives and habits of bees, and even giving us a few pointers on our play. This was a rare occurrence. I think Coach Beppe realized Aron was driving a wedge through our team.

But the damage had been done.

How could Caden and Aron play together from now on? The only second-team midfielder close to Caden's level was Logan, and he played on the left. Last season, Samantha had used Logan on the wing when Patrick had received a red card, and Logan played well. But he was not as effective on the right side, no matter the position.

Coach Beppe was right. To have any chance of advancing in the tournament, we had to work together. Aron's behavior and Caden's slump were hurting us.

Our game against Perseus Amsterdam, a team ranked nineteenth in Europe, was only three days away. We didn't have much time to fix our problems.

⚽ ⚽ ⚽

That evening, we boarded a night train to the Netherlands. The trip would be a long one, almost twelve hours, but I didn't mind. The train had a restaurant and a snack bar, and we were staying in sleeper bunks, which slept four to a room. Basically, it would be an overnight slumber party, and we'd wake up in a brand-new city.

Are you following our team's route on a map? If not, you might want to see where we are. The Czech Republic is right in the center of Europe. To get to the Netherlands, we had to go west through Germany, all the way to the sea. The Netherlands is a tiny country—probably even smaller than whatever state or country you're from—and Amsterdam is the capital. Funnily, we'd almost gone in a circle, because Amsterdam is only 220 miles from London. Though you'd have to fly or swim to get there in a straight line.

It was late in the evening when we set out from Prague. Darkness fell soon after we entered the countryside, so there wasn't much to look at. I was sharing a sleeper car with John, Eddy, and Otto. The bathroom was in the corridor outside. We could also wander down to the snack bar or stop by the other sleeper cars to see our friends.

Our narrow room had two bunk beds on either side. The bottom bunks folded down to sofas so we could relax and hang out until bedtime. After listening to music and cutting up for a while, our conversation turned more serious.

I was lying on my back with my hands behind my head. "So, what do you think happened to JoJo's gloves?"

"And our jerseys," Eddy chimed in.

"Man," John said, "this is heavy. Who'd want to hurt our team?"

I could think of no good answer.

Eddy was our DJ for the night. He was playing some hip-hop with Spanish lyrics that he turned down so we could hear each other better. "Let's think about this," he said. "Are we *positive* that's what's happening? Maybe it's just a prank," he added weakly.

Otto was working a Rubik's Cube so fast I could barely follow his movements. "A prank that could have resulted in a forfeit in the first game, and which cost us a goal in the second? No. Someone wants us to lose."

I threw up my hands. "But who? Our coaches and teammates are the only people who have been with us in both cities."

John was fiddling with the ends of his dreadlocks. It was a nervous movement I had never seen him use before. In fact, John was never nervous. "You sure about that?" he said. "Maybe there's some aggro super fan out there. One of the other teams' supporters traveling around trying to wreck everyone else. Trust me, bruvs, that happens in the Prem."

Otto shook his head. "That doesn't make sense either. We're the bottom seed in the tournament. Under that logic, someone should be trying to *help* us."

"Yeah. I guess you'ze right about that."

"Which brings us to the only logical conclusion. Someone traveling with us, for some unknown reason, is trying to sabotage us."

We all fell silent, thinking about what this meant. In the background, behind the music, I could hear the steady hum of the train chugging through the countryside.

"But who?" I said eventually. "At least we know it isn't one of us."

"True enough," John said.

Otto lifted his palms. "Do we? Maybe someone has a hidden agenda."

Eddy looked pained by the very suggestion. He was easy-going and never had anything bad to say about anyone. I knew Otto didn't really believe that one of us would do such a terrible thing. He was just so logical that, until his brain knew one hundred percent for certain who was guilty, then no one was innocent.

I might not be as book smart as Otto, but I have plenty of common sense. And I *knew* no one in our sleeper car was guilty.

Right?

I sat up straight. "Listen. This is getting serious. These pranks almost cost us both games. I doubt Coach Beppe is going to do anything, so we need to figure out who's behind this before it's too late."

"Truth, bruv," John murmured. "Who isn't happy on the squad?"

"Aron," we all said at once.

It was the obvious answer, I had to admit. "Caden," I added quietly, though I felt guilty about it. Last season, there was no love lost between us, but we had put that aside and moved on. We weren't exactly friends, but we got along okay, especially on the field. "I think he's pretty upset by his parents' divorce."

"Check," John said. "And Riley. He's a loose cannon. Remember how he stole everyone's ball in the village race?" He wagged a finger. "That's sabotage right there. With a capital S."

"Nah," I said. "Riley? I don't think so."

"Patrick too. I like that cat, but he's strange enough to pull a prank like that."

"No way. Patrick would never hurt the team."

"Maybe one of the second-team players is unhappy," Otto mused. "Then again, I would expect them to target a specific player and not the entire team. What do we know about the backup goalie?"

"I don't like this," Eddy said, looking uncomfortable. "We have to do something, but let's not start accusing people."

"Yeah," I agreed. "This will only tear us apart. Which is what whoever is doing this wants. Instead of accusing people, we should be investigating."

"How's that?" John said. "We're footballers, not detectives."

We all turned to Otto, who had just finished solving the Rubik's Cube. "What?" he said. "I don't know how to solve crimes. I suggest we keep our eyes open and try to stop any more incidents before they happen."

"Good idea," I said. "Let's watch our bags, our equipment, anything that someone could mess with."

John stuck out a fist. "Team Sherlock, right here."

We all agreed to the pact by meeting his fist bump. Soon after, we made the beds and turned out the lights, then fell asleep to the gentle movement of the train.

⚽ ⚽ ⚽

The next morning, we had an early breakfast and gazed out the windows at a flat countryside full of windmills, flowers, streams, and old barns and farmhouses. I knew almost nothing about the Netherlands, except they had a good national soccer team. I had also heard of Ajax, a famous club team in the Dutch professional league. I believe they've won the Champions League a few times.

At nine a.m., our train pulled into Amsterdam, a world capital that looked tiny in comparison to London and Paris. Those cities just go on forever. Not long after entering the city limits, our train came to a stop at the international terminal. We all rushed out to stretch our legs, then began juggling balls right there in the station while the managers sorted out our luggage.

I assumed we would take a bus or another train to our hotel, but get this: Our next ride was a boat!

After shouldering our bags, we left the train station and discovered we were right next to a river or a large canal. A yellow boat with *Taxi* on the side was waiting for us, just big enough to fit our team. Curious, we piled on board.

As we cruised through Amsterdam, I realized the entire city was full of canals and rivers. We stood at the sides of the water taxi and absorbed the sights while our pilot navigated the twisty waterways crisscrossing the city. Parks, monuments, and block after block of colorful historic buildings lined the canals. It was unlike anything I'd ever seen, and I loved the feeling of freedom on the water and the smell of the sea. I also liked how manageable Amsterdam felt, with plenty to do but small enough that my friends and I could walk around and get to know it.

Our hotel was located beside a little canal, close to a public park where we could practice. As soon as we arrived, Coach Beppe, sensing we all needed to stretch our legs, announced that practice would begin in thirty minutes.

The rooms in the cramped hotel were almost as small as the sleeper cars on the train. Otto, John, Eddy, and I were crammed together in a room again. We had a view of a canal, but the bathroom was in the hall outside, all the way at the far end.

After changing into our practice uniforms, the four of us met the others in the lobby and walked to a park full of Dutch people riding bicycles along the paths. On the far side, we found two full-size soccer fields, one of which was reserved for us.

The team managers set down the ballbags and began setting up cones as Coach Beppe asked the players to take a knee.

"Welcome to Amsterdam," he said, smiling as he rested his hands on his bulging stomach. "A city and a country with a rich tradition of football."

"Johan Cruyff and Ajax," Brock blurted out. "Total football."

Coach Beppe nodded. "That's right. In the old days, players were locked into their positions and did not have freedom to move around the field. If you were a striker, you stayed up front. If you played defense, you did not make runs down the wing or assist in midfield. The Dutch modernized the game by asking every player to be multidimensional and possess skill on the ball. That way, if a forward or a midfielder passed back to the defense, the team could retain possession."

"If the Dutch are so good," Brock said, "how come they've never won a World Cup?"

Some of the players laughed at this.

"Ah," Coach Beppe said, "it is very, very difficult to win the Cup. What is the population of this country? Quite small. They have accomplished great things on the pitch and produced many world class players. Anyway, I wanted you to be aware of the legacy of the country you are in. Now let's move to the present. As you know, Perseus Amsterdam beat Prague 1–0, and, just as we did, they lost to Paris Saint-Martin 5–1. So we have the same number of points, and the goal differential is also equal."

"Do we have to beat them to advance?" Eddy asked.

"We can tie them," Sami said. "Because we have more goals."

"He's right," Otto confirmed. "It's like the World Cup. Because we have the same record, the next tie-breaker is goal differential, and after that it's total goals scored. We scored two goals against Prague, and Amsterdam only scored one."

"True," Coach Beppe said, "but do not become complacent. The game will be very difficult. The Perseus Amsterdam players excel at all positions." He turned towards Aron and Caden. "It will take a *team* effort to beat them."

Aron sneered and looked away.

Brock flung out a hand. "What kind of a name is Perseus Amsterdam, anyway? They don't even sound like a real team."

I had wondered the same thing. Come to think of it, Ajax was also a strange name.

Riley muttered something in his Manchester accent that sounded like an insult. He and Brock slapped hands above their heads, so I guess Brock understood him. JoJo, Logan, and John also chuckled.

Otto put a hand to his forehead as if embarrassed by their actions. "Wait—you really don't know?"

The rest of us looked at him in confusion.

"Know what?" I said.

"Think about it. Ajax, Perseus, Heracles Almelo, Sparta Rotterdam?" Otto crossed his arms. "Doesn't anyone know anything about history?"

"Nope," JoJo said.

Otto threw up his arms. "Ajax? The Trojan War? *Sparta* and *Athens*?"

"Wait," Patrick said. "You tricky wicky. Those are Greek cities. Heracles—that's the dude who did the twelve tasks and killed all kinds of monsters."

I snapped my fingers. "Oh yeah—you mean Hercules? I read about that in *Percy Jackson*."

Otto gave a tragic sigh. "Hercules is the Roman name for Heracles. At least now we're getting somewhere. Heracles—that *dude*—was a demigod with superhuman strength. And Perseus was another demigod who killed Medusa, a gorgon who could turn people to stone by looking at them. The Dutch like to name their teams after famous heroes and warriors, often from Greek mythology."

"That's . . . pretty cool," I said. "Better than *FC this* and *FC that* all the time."

Brock gave me a playful shove. "You Yanks have no sense of tradition. I guess the Dutch don't either. You can't go around naming football clubs after old people in history."

"Apparently," Otto said, "you can."

⚽   ⚽   ⚽

After warmups, we ran through the same pasta drills as before, practicing our fusilli runs and our bowtie passing. Then Coach Beppe brought us together again for an announcement.

"Unfortunately," he said, "I have decided not to introduce another pasta shape to our practice today."

He looked extremely disappointed by this. The rest of us breathed a sigh of relief.

Coach Beppe folded his arms. "Instead, I have decided on a theme. *Trust*. The bees in the hive know that each member of the colony can be trusted to perform their special task without fail. So it must be with us."

After finishing his speech, he assigned partners for the rest of practice. John and I were paired together since we coordinated in the center of attack. Otto and Patrick were a team, and Brock and Eddy, and Riley and Sami.

And Caden and Aron.

I winced when Coach announced that. We all knew what he was trying to do: repair their relationship.

Good luck with that.

For the rest of practice, we focused on two-person drills with our partners, mostly two v ones in different situations. Caden and Aron performed their drills like robots. They made the plays but never spoke to each another unless forced and showed no emotion other than frowning or grimacing behind each other's backs.

Towards the end of practice, we played a game you might recognize. JoJo was in the goal, and the other five teams had to stay in the penalty box and try to score. Each team was on their own. Ten players scrambling around the box, trying to dribble and pass to their single teammate.

On the first play, Coach Beppe kicked the ball high in the air. Brock rose to head it, aiming for Eddy but sending it closer to Patrick, who took a touch but had the ball stolen by Sami. His partner, Riley, tried to get open, but John and I swarmed Sami and stole the ball.

John passed to me and made a curling run around Otto. I cut left, then right, evading two stabbing legs and trying to find a way to hit John with a pass. Finally, I lofted a ball over three players, and John smacked a header into the goal just beside JoJo's outstretched arms.

No one scored for a while after that. It was really hard to get open, and every player had to work hard to support their partner.

After half an hour of play, John and I led the pack with three goals. Otto and Patrick had two goals, as did Eddy and Brock. Riley and Sami finally managed to score when Riley slide tackled the ball away from John, and Sami poked it through JoJo's legs.

Caden and Aron had zero goals.

When Coach Beppe blew the whistle, signaling the end of the game, Aron slammed a palm against the goalpost. He started to yell at Caden, noticed Coach Beppe watching, and stalked over to his water bottle instead.

Our coach let him go, shaking his head.

At the end of practice, Coach Beppe made another announcement. Tomorrow, at the mystery training session, we would again be in pairs, but with a different partner. One of the managers ran up with a baseball cap that had everyone's name inside on a slip of paper.

Of course, Coach Beppe wouldn't give us any details about the special practice, except to say it involved a canal near our hotel.

Curious.

I watched as he pulled out two names at a time from the hat, reading them off as he went. Brock and Otto, Patrick and JoJo, Riley and Aron. The goalkeepers and second-team players were included as well.

"Leo," Coach Beppe said as he took out a slip of paper, then reached into the hat for another. "And Caden."

ENTRY #13

Do You Trust Me?

The next morning, we took a tour around Amsterdam. Oddly, Coach Beppe asked us to wear swimsuits underneath our clothes or bring them with us to change into. Did that mean the special lesson involved water?

Although the Dutch capital doesn't have the blockbuster sights of London and Paris, and is not a medieval fantasy world like Prague, I enjoyed taking water taxis down the canals, strolling over arched footbridges into different neighborhoods, and exploring the parks with my friends.

In the afternoon, we visited an outdoor museum with historic windmills that we could climb to get views of the city and the countryside. Everything was so flat and surrounded by water. I wouldn't want to be in Amsterdam during a hurricane or a tsunami.

Before dinner, we walked alongside a little canal a few blocks from our hotel. I thought Coach Beppe had forgotten about our special practice, but as we passed a wooden dock jutting into the canal, our coach stopped to talk to a tall Dutch man wearing swim trunks and a blue shirt with *Instructor* on the front. He was standing in front of a row of surfboards tied to the dock. Each of the boards had two paddles lying across it.

"Giant surfboards?" I said to no one in particular.

"Not surfboards," Aron responded. He almost never spoke unless he was yelling for the ball. "Paddleboards. We use them on lakes in Switzerland."

Coach Beppe turned to face us and rubbed his hands together. "Come, come. It is time for a little fun. Please change into your swimsuits and proceed to the dock with the partner you were assigned yesterday."

"Uh, Coach?" Riley said. I forced myself not to laugh at his faded brown-and-white swim trunks, which were much too baggy for his scrawny legs and looked like something an old grandpa would wear. "Wut are we doin'?"

"Trying to stay afloat. A difficult task with two people on a paddleboard. You will have to communicate and work together."

"But I . . ." Riley looked around, embarrassed, then spoke in a very low voice. "I can't swim."

"What?" Brock crowed. "You can't swim?"

"Shut your face."

"What do they teach you in Manchester?"

Riley muttered a string of words under his breath.

"Ah." Coach Beppe hesitated and looked at the instructor by the dock, who held up a lifejacket.

"They'll be wearing these," the instructor said with a Dutch accent. "We accommodate non-swimmers all the time. And the canal is quite shallow. He can stand if he needs. I don't advise drinking the water, but he'll be safe if he falls."

Aron stepped forward. "He's my partner, and I'm an expert paddleboarder. I won't let him fall. But if he does, I'll jump in with him. I'm also a certified lifeguard."

I rolled my eyes, not even surprised that Aron was an expert paddleboarder *and* a trained lifeguard.

"Riley?" Coach Beppe said. "What do you say? I'll leave the choice to participate to you."

When Riley hesitated, Brock began to flap his arms, walk in a circle, and cluck like a chicken. I elbowed him in the side at the same time JoJo smacked the back of his head.

"Yeah, okay," Riley said with a sullen expression. "I'll do it."

"Well done," Coach Beppe said. "We are already facing our fears today. Is there anyone else who cannot swim?"

No one spoke.

"And does anyone besides Aron have experience with a paddleboard?"

There was still no response, which relieved me. I had never even seen a paddleboard.

"In that case," Coach Beppe said, "the lesson will be quite poignant. Mr. Vandemark will impart some instructions, and each team will do their best to navigate to the end of the canal and back. The scenery along the way is lovely, but you will have to work together to stay in sync. If you don't, you will lose your balance and fall. Teamwork, Knights. You must trust each other."

The temperature had been scorching hot all day. Though still humid, it was starting to cool off, and it felt good to strip down to my swim trunks and put on a life vest. After everyone had changed clothes, I waited eagerly for my turn, not bothering to listen to Mr. Vandemark's short lesson on paddleboarding.

I mean, how hard could it be?

"Wait," JoJo said. "Coach Bep, what's this got to do with football?"

Our coach was watching from the bank of the canal with an amused smile. "Everything."

Mr. Vandemark untied the first paddleboard in line and held it steady. Aron volunteered for him and Riley to go first. Aron stepped on smoothly, picked up a paddle, and watched Riley creep gingerly onto the paddleboard. It rocked a little, which Aron adjusted to by getting low, spreading his legs, and balancing his arms and the paddle.

"Ha!" Riley said smugly as he picked up the second paddle and held it over his head. "Simple."

Brock snickered. "Yeah, thanks to Aron."

It was our turn next. "You ready?" I asked Caden as we met on the dock.

He shrugged and didn't answer, clearly not interested in the experience.

"Here we go, lads," Mr. Vandemark said, holding the edge of the board as I walked on, bent to pick up the paddle, and stood up straight.

Easy, just like I thought.

After Caden came on board and took the front position, Mr. Vandemark asked if we had any questions.

"Nope," I said confidently, eager to get going. It looked fun to stand and paddle smoothly down the canal like Aron and Riley were doing. "Let's go."

Mr. Vandemark shoved our paddleboard off the dock. As soon as he did, our board began to wobble. Caden and I tried to make it stop, but our actions only seemed to make it worse. Mr. Vandemark was shouting instructions, but it was too late. Caden and I fell off the side of the paddleboard and plunged into the murky green waters of the canal.

Our lifejackets kept us afloat. The water was cool and felt good, though I couldn't see the bottom, which made me nervous. There could be all kinds of slimy, creepy things down there.

Far worse, however, was the roasts and trash talk our teammates rained down on us.

Brock howled with glee. "A couple of wet dogs right there. Good job, Yank!"

"Alright, Leo!" John said, holding his sides as he doubled over with laughter. "You'ze all wet, bruv!"

Sheepish, I tried to climb back onto the paddleboard with Caden, but we couldn't stabilize the annoying thing. It kept rocking back and forth so much that we couldn't seem to climb on. That board had a mind of its own, I tell you.

Mr. Vandemark had to jump in the water and hold the paddleboard. "Let's try this again," the instructor said. "Remember: feet parallel and a few feet apart. Center yourself on the board. Toes forward, knees slightly bent, back straight. Head and shoulders up, shift your weight at your hips. Good!" he said as Caden and I climbed on and found our balance. "I'll push you more slowly this time."

The paddleboard wobbled again as it slid through the water. This time, Caden and I followed the instructions and managed to keep standing.

"We're doing it!" I said. "Um, now what?"

"Time your strokes," the instructor called out. "The person in the lead is the rhythm paddler. That's you, Caden. Decide on a number of strokes per side—I suggest three or four—then switch."

"How many strokes do you want?" I asked Caden.

"Let's do three."

"Okay."

Caden dipped his oar in the water and took a stroke. I tried to match him, but my timing wasn't perfect, and the paddleboard began to wobble.

"Careful," he snapped.

"Okay," I said. "Take it easy."

"I don't want to fall again."

"You think I do?"

Slowly, carefully, we began to find our rhythm. Ahead of us, Riley and Aron were moving steadily forward, far ahead in the canal. I glanced back and saw the other paddleboards moving forward in a line. No one else seemed to have fallen, but they all looked wobbly.

It wasn't easy. Caden and I had to stay in constant communication. But eventually we made some progress, and I enjoyed the experience, though I didn't get to relax as much as I wanted, since I was concentrating so hard on staying afloat.

Riley and Aron had already turned around. As they passed us, Riley tried to break our concentration by splashing water on us with his paddle and tossing a few insults, cackling the entire time. Aron kept paddling like a machine.

When we reached the end of the canal, we made a careful U-turn, using the wall for support, and headed back the way we had come. By this time, Caden and I had developed a nice partnership. Three strokes on the left, three strokes on the right. He wasn't even calling out the numbers anymore.

"Ready for the game tomorrow?" I asked when I thought we could safely talk without falling.

"Sure," he mumbled.

"That wasn't very convincing."

"Just paddle and leave me alone, Leo."

After a moment, I said, "I've been meaning to tell you I'm sorry about your parents."

His head whipped around, blond hair flying, almost causing us to capsize. "How do you know about that?"

"I . . . well, everyone knows. I don't remember who told me."

"Yeah, well, whatever," he muttered.

I didn't know very much about divorce. I knew some other people my age whose parents had split up, but none of my close friends. "Do you have to . . . move out or anything?"

"My dad's leaving. I'm staying with my mum and my brother. I tried to move in with Logan, but his parents said no. They don't even want me around anymore," he said bitterly. "They think I'm a bad influence now."

That shocked me. All last season, Caden and Logan had been best friends. This summer, even though they paired up sometimes, I had noticed they weren't talking very much. That must be hard for Caden to deal with, on top of his parents' divorce. No wonder he wasn't as motivated. When my mom died, I channeled all that anger and disappointment onto the soccer field, but I suppose some people deal with grief in different ways.

"I know what you're thinking," he said. "That I've lost my focus. It's true, you know. I guess I'm just . . . angry. At my parents. At myself. What did I do wrong? It's not like things were ever that great at home before," he muttered, "but at least Dad was there."

"I'm sorry," I said again, not knowing what else to say. I sensed Caden just needed someone to listen.

"I'll play better," he said firmly. "Promise. Starting tomorrow."

"Good. We need you."

"I don't know if I can play with Aron, though. I just want to punch that wallybag."

I wasn't sure what a wallybag was, but I could use my imagination. "That would only hurt the team. I know he's being a jerk, but let me talk to him, okay?"

"That won't help. We can't play together, Leo."

But you have to, I thought. *Or we'll lose.*

We ended the conversation as we approached the dock. Thankful we had finished without plunging into the canal again, I let my guard down too soon and almost fell as I stepped off the paddleboard. Riley, who was sitting on the edge of the dock with his legs dangling into the water, grew very excited when I almost slipped, and groaned in disappointment when I caught myself.

As I stepped onto solid ground, I noticed Coach Beppe watching me and Caden, then glancing away when I caught him looking.

It made me wonder if those names he pulled out of the hat had been random after all.

⚽ ⚽ ⚽

On the walk back to the hotel, everyone seemed to be in a good mood except Aron and Caden. I doubted that standup paddleboard lessons, like pasta and beehives, would have any effect on our performance, but at least we were ready to play.

Our game was scheduled for 9 a.m. the next morning. The stadium was half an hour away. Because of the early start—we also had to eat breakfast and warm up—Coach Beppe wanted the lights out by ten. He asked the hotel reception to give everyone a wakeup call at 6 a.m.

I did my best to fall asleep on time, but it took me awhile to drift off. The next thing I knew, someone was shaking me and calling my name.

"Leo," Otto said in an urgent voice. "Leo, wake up!"

Still groggy, I pushed to a sitting position and yawned. "Take it easy. I'm awake. I didn't even hear the alarm. Did it just go off?"

"No. That's the problem. It *never* went off. Nobody's did. Not even Coach Beppe's. A manager just called and said it's eight o'clock and the middle of rush hour. We have to leave *now*. If traffic gets any worse, we might miss the game!"

ENTRY #14

Perseus Amsterdam

I jumped out of bed, pulled on my silver-and-black shorts and jersey, slipped into my flip-flops, and threw everything else into my duffel bag. John and Eddy were doing the same. I didn't even stop to brush my teeth or drink a glass of water.

Otto threw open the door. The four of us rushed outside. We found a manager waiting in the hall, windmilling his arms, shepherding us towards the elevator. "Go go go!" he cried.

The elevator light was on, but it stopped six floors above us. "Take the stairs instead!"

Brock and Riley burst out of their room looking as messy as we did. All of us bolted for the stairs, took them two at a time, and poured into the lobby. Coach Beppe was already there, checking his watch, as nervous as I'd ever seen him.

Within minutes, everyone was downstairs. We raced outside, saw a line of three vans waiting by the curb, and jumped in.

This was an utter disaster. On the way to the stadium, a manager in our van handed out snack bars, apples, and bottles of water. At least we had something in our belly. Traffic was awful, and everyone kept staring at the clock on the dashboard as the driver of the van did his best to navigate through the crowded city.

8:30.

8:45.

8:55.

Right at 9 a.m.—when the game was supposed to start—we sprinted through the front entrance of the youth stadium. All the fans were staring at us, no doubt wondering what had happened.

Coach Beppe, huffing and puffing as he ran, looked more like a penguin with arms than a former star player. He went straight to the refs, pleading our case while we threw on our socks and cleats. The players on Perseus Amsterdam, dressed in bright orange uniforms with black socks, shook their heads in annoyance at the delay.

"Okay!" Coach Beppe called out as he hurried to our bench. "We can play, but it's time to start. No warmups, I'm afraid. We were lucky the referee was merciful. Same lineup as last time. Fusilli, bowtie, bees, trust!"

I ran out to my position, throwing my knees high, waving my arms in circles, trying to get loose. I knew the stadium was full of fans but didn't have time to process the details. All I saw was a clear blue sky, a scoreboard with *Knights* and *Perseus*, and bleachers filled with a surprising number of people. Hundreds, maybe a thousand.

My stomach rumbled, wondering where the rest of its breakfast was. That was okay. I could eat later.

The referee blew the whistle.

Game on!

Knowing we had no time to stretch or warmup, the Perseus players pressed the attack, taking the ball down the middle. I didn't blame them. We were the ones who had shown up late.

Before the whistle blew, I still felt as if I'd rolled out of bed.

But now my adrenaline snapped me awake. Good thing too. There was no time to ease into the game. This was the Tournament of Champions. I had to play my very best, right this very second, and keep it up the whole game.

I stepped up to defend their number 10. He was a small player, even shorter and wirier than I was, with a long nose, curly brown hair that fell to his shoulders, and a skinny ratlike face. For once, I might be able to push my opponent around.

He dribbled towards me. I put one foot in front of the other, in a proper defensive stance, not giving an inch. He started to pass the ball to his right—then whipped the ball to his left at the last moment, pushing it by me with a quick one-two.

Startled by the move and surprised by his quickness, I lunged for the ball and missed. He blew by me and headed downfield, free to carve open our defense.

Wow. I had misjudged that one. He was going to be a handful.

I chased after him. *Burg*, the back of his jersey read. As I watched in dismay, Burg dribbled past Brock as well, using an inside stepover and again going to his left. Brock tried to ram him with his shoulder, but Burg slid past him like he was coated in oil.

Their wingers raced downfield, calling for the ball. Riley ran over to help but he was too late. Burg took another dribble and rocketed a shot across his body at the top left corner. JoJo jumped too late to make the save, but the ball clanged off the crossbar and out of bounds.

Whew. We had dodged a bullet on the first play of the game.

After Burg took the shot, he stood and faced our goal,

pointing a finger at JoJo. "Wait—a girl?" he said, loud enough for everyone to hear. "You have a girl for a goalie?"

"Yeah," Brock said, getting in his face. "What of it?"

Burg laughed, though he wisely backed away with his hands up.

"You better get back," Brock said.

JoJo was staring at Burg with venom in her eyes. She spat on the ground, turned, retrieved the ball, and sent the goal kick past the midfield line, farther than I'd ever seen her kick.

After surviving the initial attack, we grew into the game. Perseus Amsterdam was a very, very good team. Just as Coach Beppe said, all of their players were comfortable with the ball. Burg was their best player, or at least their best attacker. He was a whirlwind, racing all over the field, using his quick feet to sneak past defenders and find the open player.

Ten minutes into the game, a Perseus winger flew down the left sideline, trying to beat Sami. It was a close race, but Sami covered his position well. The winger was unable to cross the ball. Instead, he cut back hard, trying to dribble inside. Sami lunged out with a leg to stop him, then cried out in pain and fell to the ground.

Left by himself, the winger took advantage and drove hard to the goal. Just before he took a shot, Riley came out of nowhere and slide tackled him, poking the ball across the end line.

The referee blew the whistle to stop play. Sami was still on the ground, holding the back of his leg with both hands. I ran over to check on him.

"I think I pulled something," he said, gasping in pain.

Our trainer came out to probe Sami's leg. Eventually Sami

stood on his own but had to leave the game, limping off the field with one arm around the trainer and another around Brock. When Coach Beppe sent in a second-team player to replace Sami, Otto and I exchanged a look of concern. I knew exactly what he was thinking.

One: We hoped Sami was okay.

Two: Not only had the missed alarms almost caused us to forfeit the game, but the quick start with no warmups probably led to Sami's injury.

There was no time to dwell on it. The game restarted, and I was getting an increasingly bad feeling about the outcome. Caden was playing a little better, making sharp passes and good turns, but he and Aron weren't communicating. At all. Caden kept choosing to pass to me or John or Patrick—anyone but Aron—and it was obviously on purpose. Aron was fuming, stalking back and forth on the wing, yelling for the ball.

The next time Burg came at me, I played better defense and forced him to pass. But once he did, I lost him on his run, and he received the ball near the edge of the penalty box. As Brock and Riley closed in, Burg saw a gap and took a hard shot on goal, a knuckleball that curved away from JoJo, causing me to suck in a breath.

She dove and smacked the ball away. "That all you got?" she said with a sneer.

The next time Perseus attacked, she made another diving save, and then another.

I bet Burg wished he had kept his mouth shut.

Right before halftime, disaster struck. Burg took a corner kick that sailed into the box. A couple of players touched the ball, but no one could control it. Eddy tried to clear the ball, but his kick hit Caden in the leg, bounced backwards, and slipped into the goal.

As JoJo banged her palm against the goalpost, Aron turned on Caden and said, "What are you doing? You just cost us a goal!"

"Hey!" I said, running over to separate them. "That wasn't his fault. It could have happened to anyone."

"But it didn't," Aron said. "This guy is killing us."

As he ran off, I put an arm around Caden's shoulder. "It wasn't your fault."

He put his head in his hands. "Yes. It was."

"Like I said, it could have been anyone."

"I'm poison, Leo. It's all my fault."

I had a feeling he was talking about more than soccer.

The halftime whistle blew. Dejected by the freak goal, our team walked slowly off the field with our heads down. Coach Beppe gave a nice speech to raise our spirits, but it was JoJo who got us pumped again.

"We're not gonna let these little orange carrots beat us, are we?" she said. "C'mon! If we lose, we go home. I want to see more cities. Before I joined this team, I'd never even left South London."

I held out a palm, determined to play better. "I don't want to go home either."

John put his hand on top of mine. "Let's do this, bruvs."

Everyone joined in. We roared our team name and retook the field, determined to fight back.

The second half started better. We kept possession and had Perseus on their heels. Otto, Caden, and I controlled the midfield, while Eddy made a lot of good runs to support us.

But we had trouble getting shots, and one of the main reasons why was the lack of teamwork between Caden and Aron. That was putting it nicely. They were at each other's throats the entire game, and our opponents knew it. Caden did start passing to Aron, but not enough, and the Perseus defenders focused more on everyone else, which made it hard for John and Patrick to find space.

I knew something had to be done about Caden and Aron by the time our next game rolled around. But if we didn't figure out something real fast in *this* game, there wouldn't be another one.

I took this as a personal challenge. Their defense was shutting John and Patrick down, and so far, Burg had outplayed me.

I had to do better.

Soon after, I got my chance. Eddy made a great defensive play and stripped the ball from their right winger. In a flash, Eddy sent a ball through the middle, leading me with a perfect pass. I took the ball in stride and pressed upfield.

Burg stepped up. I had not forgotten the first play of the game, when he had beaten me one on one. It was time to return the favor.

As he closed in, I stutter-stepped with my left foot, keeping my right toe on the ball. Burg took the bait and lunged in. Once he did, I spun around him, keeping the ball on my right foot the entire time, using my body to shield him off. He had extremely quick feet and tried to stab the ball through my legs.

But my feet were even quicker. I kept the ball just out of reach, using my body as a shield, then surged forward, leaving Burg struggling to catch up.

I took in the field with a glance. My teammates raced forward, ready to break behind enemy lines. Their defense was playing off Aron, maybe thinking we had not used him very much because he was a weak player. I took advantage and lofted the ball over the defense, leading him towards the goal. Then I followed my own pass.

Eager for the opportunity, Aron raced forward, beating his defender to the ball by half a step. But my tough pass had rolled too far forward, leaving Aron with a poor angle on goal. I thought he would take the shot anyway, because he was a ball hog, but instead he used a back heel to return the ball to me.

The sneaky pass caught everyone off guard. Me included. I wasn't even sure how Aron knew I was trailing him. Maybe he just guessed. But I recovered and hit the perfect pass in stride, a one-touch bullet that screamed into the bottom right corner.

Goal!

Except it wasn't. As we began to celebrate, I heard an awful sound: the snap of a referee's flag.

Aron must have been a fraction offside before he received my pass.

Argh! The most frustrating play in the world is to have a goal called back due to offside. But the lead referee agreed. My goal didn't count.

And Perseus Amsterdam had the ball.

Less than ten minutes to go. We were still losing 1–0. We had fought hard, but I began to lose hope. With our attack on the right so weakened, how could we break through?

Perseus made another push. Riley broke up the play, and Brock launched the ball downfield. Patrick tried a cross that sailed over Aron's head and out of bounds. Burg received the throw-in and tried to beat me again, but I had figured out he preferred to go left. I stripped the ball and passed to Otto. In the second half, I had outplayed Burg and could tell he was frustrated.

But my little victory wouldn't tie the game for us.

Sensing defeat, knowing time was almost up, John drove the ball deep into the penalty box and managed to win a corner kick. The referee checked his watch. This might be the last play of the game. Caden ran over to take the kick, and I stood just outside the box, bouncing on the balls of my feet, ready for anything. Everyone came forward to fight for position, including Eddy and Brock and Riley.

Caden sent in a high, lofting ball. It hung in the air before plummeting like a falling star. One of the Perseus players tried to head the ball out, but it didn't go very far. Two players collided. The ball hit the ground and bounced. No whistle. I raced inside, trying to help out. There was a mad scramble for the ball. I couldn't even see it, just a tangle of arms and legs. I smelled dirt and grass and sweat from all the players. Finally, the ball popped loose, and my heart sank. It was rolling towards the edge of the penalty box, and a Perseus defender was about to boot it away and end the game, securing their victory and our exit from the tournament.

Then, in the corner of my eye, a blur passed by, and I couldn't believe what happened next.

ENTRY #15

Four Suspects and a Train to Germany

At first, I thought a giant banana with legs had rushed the field. Or maybe a fan wearing a yellow shirt.

Then I realized it was JoJo in her bright goalie jersey, sprinting towards the ball rolling through the penalty box. She must have raced all the way upfield for the corner kick, knowing it didn't matter if she got caught out of position because it was surely the last play of the game.

No one was marking her. She had caught everyone, including her own teammates, by surprise. With the goal looming, JoJo plowed through the crowd of players and struck the ball hard with her right toe.

Wait—a toe ball?

I winced.

Please, *please* never kick the ball with your toe. It's impossible to control. The rest of JoJo's form was terrible too. It was obvious she didn't know how to plant her foot in the right position, lean over the ball, balance her body, and strike with her laces. I know she's a goalie, but her form was so bad I wondered if she had ever taken a shot before.

Ninety-nine times out of one hundred, that toe-poke was going in the stands. Or anywhere but on target.

But this time, JoJo's wild toe ball whipped through the

crowd of players, somehow avoiding a deflection, and splashed the net in the right side of the goal. The Perseus Amsterdam keeper had drifted to the left, worried about John and Patrick, and didn't see JoJo's shot until it was too late.

The home crowd fell silent, and the players on both teams watched, stunned, as the ball bounced and then settled in the goal.

The referee blew the whistle to signal the end of the game. The final score was 1–1. We had tied Perseus Amsterdam, which meant we were advancing to the knockout rounds!

As our team started celebrating and our opponents hung their heads, JoJo ran straight to Burg, put a finger in his face, and began shouting.

"How 'bout that, yeah? You like that, cheeseburger? A *girl* just won the game. Beat your sorry team at the last second. What's that? Got nothing to say? Want some fries with that loss, cheeseburger? Whatcha think about girls playing now? Huh? Huh? Cat got your tongue?"

Burg shuffled his feet and tried to walk away, but JoJo followed him and kept throwing barbs. Wow, she was mad. I ran over to intervene before she started a fight or got a red card and missed the next game. She pushed me away and kept going after Burg. Then Brock and John got between them, and the rest of my teammates helped out, surrounding JoJo so she had nowhere to go. At last, the wild light in her eyes dimmed and she thrust a gloved fist in the air.

We chanted her name and whooped in celebration.

⚽ ⚽ ⚽

After the game, in our locker room inside the Perseus Amsterdam youth stadium, our victory party continued. We were the underdogs of the whole tournament. I could hardly believe we had just advanced to the knockout rounds. Winning the trophy still seemed like an impossible dream, but at least that dream was alive.

"Yo, Coach Bep!" JoJo said, still glowing from her miracle toe-poke that had sent us through. "Who we playing next?"

"Let us check," he said. "The draw takes place immediately after the group stage. Hold on."

We all held our breath while he consulted his phone. Like the World Cup, the knockout rounds of the Tournament of Champions were single elimination. One loss and you went home.

Unlike the World Cup, the knockout round brackets for our tournament were determined by a random draw. That meant we could be playing any of the teams who advanced, including Paris Saint-Martin.

Coach Beppe looked up. "RB Munich."

Hearing the name of our next opponent caused us to break into another cheer.

"Are we in PSM's bracket?" Brock asked. "Who's next after Munich?"

Coach Beppe chuckled. "Patience, young bees. We are not in Paris Saint-Martin's bracket. And you should only worry about your next opponent, *sí*?" He clapped his hands and spread his palms. "The game with Munich is days away, which doesn't leave us much time. Relax. Sleep. Recover. I'll let you know our travel plans as soon as I can."

As the celebration wound down, I noticed Aron in a corner of the locker room, taking off his socks and cleats by himself, hanging his head. I assumed he was thinking about my goal that had not counted because he was offside. I headed over to tell him not to worry about it, but Caden arrived first.

"You're a lucky guy," Caden said with a nasty grin. "If JoJo hadn't scored, your offside would've cost us the match."

Aron snarled. "Only because your stupid own goal gave them the lead."

"That was an unlucky bounce. I had nothing to do with it and you know it. Your offside was just lazy."

As Aron flew to his feet, I rushed over to stand between them. I tried to calm them down, but they both left the locker room in a huff, angrier than ever.

⚽ ⚽ ⚽

After lunch at the hotel, Coach Beppe announced we would be taking a train to Munich—that's a city in Germany—at 10 a.m. the next morning. The journey would take around nine hours, which meant we wouldn't arrive until the following evening. That only gave us one full day in Munich before the game.

Like Coach Beppe had suggested, we spent the rest of the day lounging at the hotel and in a nearby park. One piece of good news: Sami's injury was not as bad as everyone thought. He should be ready to play the next game. That was a huge relief. RB Munich was the eleventh seed in the tournament, so we would need every bit of help we could get.

Which made me wonder what Coach Beppe planned to do about Caden and Aron. Something had to change. Munich was an even stronger team, at least in the rankings, than Perseus Amsterdam. We couldn't afford to have our right-side attack weakened by a feud between our players.

⚽ ⚽ ⚽

The next morning, after breakfast, Coach Beppe asked me, John, Otto, and Eddy to stay with him for a minute. Wondering what he wanted, the four of us took a seat at his table and watched him pour a packet of sugar into his espresso. Coach Beppe had a pained expression. I wondered if he wanted to talk about Caden or Aron, maybe ask our advice on how to repair their relationship.

"Young men," Coach Beppe said, setting his forearms heavily on the table, "I am sorry to have this conversation, but something has come to light we need to discuss."

The four of us exchanged a confused look.

"What gives, Coach?" John said.

Coach Beppe interlaced his fingers. "Before breakfast, I talked to the hotel manager. It appears that someone made a call to Reception the night before the game and canceled the wake-up calls. All of them."

I assumed something like this had happened.

But who would do such a thing?

"So who was it?" Eddy said, echoing my thoughts.

Coach Beppe's expression turned grave. "The caller used my name. Obviously, I did no such thing. The manager was able to check the caller ID, and I'm told the call came from the room where the four of you are staying."

Okay. Now *that* surprised me.

"But Coach," I said, glancing at my teammates and seeing the same shock on their faces I was feeling. "None of us would have done that."

Coach Beppe took a sip of espresso. "To be honest, I don't think so either." He opened his palms. "But at this point I don't know *what* to think. This is the only clue we have, so I must put you on notice and tell you that we are watching the four of you closely."

I sank down in my chair, feeling very small.

"I have to ask something else," Coach Beppe said. "Were any of you alone in the room at any time? Or do you remember someone else being alone?"

For a long moment, no one spoke. He was asking us to rat each other out. I couldn't remember anyone being alone, but even if I could, I wouldn't have said anything. My loyalty to my friends was strong and I just couldn't believe one of them was guilty.

"I was," John said.

Coach Beppe set his espresso down.

"I went up first after dinner that night," John continued. "I was alone for a minute."

"That's when the call went through," Coach Beppe said quietly. "Right after dinner."

"But I didn't make that call! I'd never hurt the team."

All of a sudden, I remembered John fiddling with his hair when we were discussing who the traitor might be, and thinking he was nervous about something. *Oh no*, I thought. *It can't be John. Besides, he wouldn't tell on himself, would he?*

I didn't believe it for a second.

Otto leaned forward. "Did you leave the room? At any time?"

At first, I was annoyed with Otto, thinking he was also accusing John.

Then I understood what Otto was thinking.

"Yeah," John said. "I went to the restroom. There's only two room cards, and you blokes had 'em. I left the door propped open and hustled back."

Otto leaned back and crossed his arms. "That's what happened. Someone—the traitor—followed John to our room and made the call so they could blame it on one of us. They knew someone would check the call log and trace it back."

Coach Beppe took another sip of espresso and nodded thoughtfully to show he was considering the theory.

But he didn't say that he agreed.

⚽ ⚽ ⚽

The train to Munich was sleek and fast but did not have four-person sections like the other trains. The seating was more like a bus, with two-person rows and big windows. I sat next to Brock this time. The sky was gray and gloomy and threatening to rain. By the time we entered Germany—only a few hours from Amsterdam—a downpour had started, so there was nothing much to see outside the window.

We still had a long way to go. Germany is a huge country, at least compared to the Netherlands, and Munich was all the way on the other side.

So far, Brock had been asleep and snoring like a buffalo. When we stopped at a station in the middle of the country so people could board and depart, he woke up and looked out the window. It was still pouring rain. "Are we there?"

"We have six hours left," I said.

"Blech."

"I know. This journey's kinda boring. At least we have Wi-Fi."

Brock grunted. He wasn't much of a gamer. As the new passengers settled in and the train started moving, he said, "I heard about the call from your room."

I set down my device. "Who told you? I was going to, but you've been sleeping since we left."

He waved a hand. "One of the second teamers heard Coach Beppe talking to a manager about it. They told Logan, and he told me and Riley. Everyone knows. It's a problem."

"Yeah. I know."

He turned to face me, squinting his beady eyes and lowering his voice. "I never thought I'd say this about a Yank, but you're the only person I can trust for sure on this team."

"I trust you too. But I also trust, well, everyone else. I don't think *anyone* would try to sabotage us."

"But someone is. That's a fact."

"I guess you're right," I murmured. "But definitely not Otto, John, or Eddy. No way."

"So who made that call?"

When I told him that John had gone to the bathroom and left the door cracked, leaving the room empty, Brock grunted. "Yeah, I guess that changes things. It could be anyone. Well, not anyone. Someone who wants to frame someone in your room. So, who has a beef with one of you four?"

I had been thinking about that same question.

"I think it's Caden," he said. "You took his spot last year. His number too. Maybe he's still bitter. And he's been cranky all summer."

"He's cranky because his parents are getting a divorce." I shook my head. "Caden's okay. And he wants to win."

"Maybe. I hate to say it, but Aron's right about one thing. Caden's playing like trash." He poked me in the chest. "You know me, Yank. I like to win. And I didn't come here to play in the second division. You gotta figure something out."

"Me?"

"Yeah, you. Haven't you been paying attention? The team listens to you. I just knock people around. And all Coach Beppe does is talk about bees and pasta. The guy's a legend, but he's retired now and doesn't care about this tournament."

⚽ ⚽ ⚽

I listened to music and dozed for the rest of the trip. The rain never let up, so I couldn't tell you much about Munich as we pulled into the train station. All I knew was the city seemed big, wet, and grey.

A bus took us to a tall modern hotel with neon lights. It was dusk when we arrived. Too late to practice or see the city. Everyone's legs, mine included, were cramped from the long journey. After dinner, desperate for some exercise, we all put on our swimming trunks and hit the indoor pool on the tenth floor. There was no diving board, but we amused ourselves playing keep-away with a beach ball.

A couple of hours later, feeling better, we returned to our rooms for bed. I was sharing a triple with John and Eddy. We vowed not to leave the door unlocked.

⚽ ⚽ ⚽

By the next morning, a Wednesday, the thunderstorms had finally stopped. The day was cloudy and cool but at least we could practice. After breakfast, grateful to be outside, we walked two blocks to a turf field that belonged to a college. The field was surrounded by brick and concrete buildings. Above them, I could see the tops of glass office towers in the distance. It reminded me a little of the Cage in London, except this was a full-size field.

"Ah," Coach Beppe said as we gathered around him. "At last we can stretch our legs. Our game is tomorrow morning so we will not push too hard. Let us hope we do not have any more missing jerseys, slippery gloves, or underused alarm clocks." He crossed his meaty arms as if to reinforce his words.

As promised, we had an easy practice and ran through the same drills we already knew. Fusilli and bowties and trust-building runs with a partner. In the light scrimmage, Coach Beppe made a change to the lineup: he moved Otto to right midfield and Caden to the left.

It was a smart but risky move. Otto would be fine. Like me, he could use both feet and had played right midfield on his old team. But as far as I knew, Caden had never played on the left.

Logan hung his head in disappointment, and I didn't blame him. He was a proven left-midfielder and Caden wasn't, so it was a slap in the face to choose Caden. It meant Coach Beppe thought Caden, even on his weaker side, was better than Logan.

After practice, we sat with our water bottles on the bench while Coach Beppe taught us a little about the history of German soccer. I knew Germany had a solid national team, but I didn't know just how good: They were tied with Italy for the second-most World Cup titles—four—of any country. Only Brazil had more. But Germany had reached the finals eight times—even more than Brazil!

As you probably know, Bayern Munich is one of the best club teams in the world. They play in the Bundesliga along with Borussia Dortmund, another team I like. Coach Beppe told us the Bundesliga has the highest average attendance of any league in the world. Soccer is popular in Germany!

I raised a hand. "What do you know about RB Munich?"

"I haven't seen their U14s play," Coach Beppe said, "but their scouting report is similar to most German teams: skilled, physical, and excellent team players. They might not beat you on the dribble, but they will delight in passing around you." He wagged a finger. "Outstanding students of the bees, they are."

"Isn't their current formation a 3–1–4–2?" Otto asked.

"Correct."

"I've heard their coach is a tactical genius."

"Is that so?" Coach Beppe said in a disinterested voice.

"Their best player is a defensive mid, and their two strikers led the league in goals. First and second place."

"Hmm. Most impressive."

Otto's large forehead wrinkled in frustration. "Well? We've never faced a 3–1–4–2. How should we play against them?"

"As I've said before, the same way we always play." Coach Beppe stroked his chin and seesawed his head back and forth, as if contemplating something. "In this particular situation, perhaps I can impart some advice on how to adjust to their tactics."

Finally, I thought. *Some actual knowledge!*

"But first," he said, patting his belly, "it is time for a little sightseeing and our special practice. And, more importantly, for lunch."

ENTRY #16

Human Checkers

After a late lunch, the team managers took us on a whirlwind tour of Munich. I wasn't sure what happened to Coach Beppe and the special practice. Maybe he got distracted by a bumblebee.

We didn't have time for much. We didn't even go inside any buildings, though we walked past a ton of world-class museums and cathedrals and that sort of thing. To be honest, I didn't mind. I had seen plenty of those. Mostly I thought about the next game and talked to my friends, though I'll admit I was impressed by how modern Munich felt. Everything was clean and well organized. Public transport was everywhere. Trains, buses, a subway, and even a tram system, which is like a small bus-train that runs through the city. Everything was comfortable and easy to ride.

The last stop on the tour was my favorite. It was a huge public square called the Marienplatz, right in the center of town. We have a public square like that in Middleton, but the Marienplatz is about a thousand times bigger and made of stones that are probably a thousand years old. It's filled with people and food vendors and street performers, and surrounded by historic buildings that reminded me of Prague (though not *that* impressive).

The day was sunny and so clear that we could see, in the

distance, the hazy outline of a mountain range. Otto told us those are the Alps.

In the middle of the Marienplatz, beside a statue of a woman, was a life-size chessboard made of marble squares. When I say *life-size*, I mean the squares were big enough for a person to stand on, and all of the chess pieces were two feet tall. The pieces were lined up on either side of the empty board. I assumed you were supposed to set them up and move them around.

"Good evening," a familiar voice called out from behind us.

I looked up and saw Coach Beppe emerge from the crowd, walk to the chessboard, and step right onto it. He gestured for us to join him.

"What's he doing?" Eddy whispered.

I shrugged. "No idea."

As we all walked onto the marble board, confused, Coach Beppe smiled. "Welcome to our afternoon practice. Chess is a favorite pastime of mine and has many parallels to football. But so does an even simpler game. Today you will test your mettle against your humble coach in a game of human checkers."

A ripple of confused excitement ran through the team.

"He's gone truly mental," Riley said. "Stark raving barmy."

"Who would like to play first?" Coach Beppe asked.

To my surprise, Brock raised a hand. "I know how to play checkers. I beat my cousins all the time."

"Well then, brave lad, step right up." Coach Beppe walked behind the last row on one side of the chessboard. He opened a palm towards Brock, inviting him to stand on the opposite side. Once Brock was in position, Coach Beppe turned to the rest of us. "Everyone, please take a black square in the first three rows on both sides. Come, come. Don't be shy."

I hesitated, then stepped onto a square in the middle of the last row on Brock's side. You know how to play checkers, right? You move diagonally across the board, staying on the same color squares, trying to jump and capture all of your opponent's pieces? I had played lots of checkers, mostly with my mom and Aunt Janice. I was pretty good and felt certain I could beat Brock and probably Coach Beppe.

Each side had three rows of four checkers, or in this case, people acting as checkers. That's twelve people on each side. Our team has twenty-four players, including our goalies. Since Brock was playing against Coach Beppe, one of the managers took the final position.

Coach Beppe rubbed his hands together and let his opponent make the first move. It was funny to watch Brock bark out an order and force Riley to move around the board.

Coach Beppe moved JoJo to the next row, and so on and so on. About twenty moves later, it was clear that a slaughter was in process.

And Brock was not on the winning side.

"Geez," he grumbled as Coach Beppe took yet another of his 'pieces,' forcing Caden off the board. "I didn't know you were a checkers master."

"Just a student of the game," Coach Beppe replied. After the destruction was finished, he held out a palm and said mildly, "Next?"

Three more players tried their luck: Patrick, Aron, and Sami.

And three more annihilations took place.

"Yo, Coach is good," John said as we shuffled off the board after being double-jumped by Logan.

"Yeah," I said, "but I bet I know who can beat him." I turned to Otto, who was still on the board. "You play checkers, don't you?"

"All of my life."

"You're probably the best player in Hungary, aren't you? As good as I am at FIFA?"

"I don't know about that." Otto folded his arms with a confident expression. "But I am very, very good."

Before the next game, Coach Beppe gathered us at one end of the board and spoke to us from the center. "You might be wondering why we are here. The game of football, you see, has many similarities to checkers. Tactics are important, yes, but *strategy* is equally so. Do you know the difference? Tactics are short-term moves. A passing scheme, a dribbling maneuver, or even the formation you line up with. Strategies, on the other hand, are principles that apply to all situations. What is important in checkers? Controlling the middle of the board, the same as in football. Creating overloads and imbalances with superior numbers. Using your strengths. Identifying weak spots in your opponent. Remember these principles as we continue to play, then think about how they apply to the pitch."

"What about the 3–1–4–2?" Otto asked.

Coach Beppe blinked. "But I have just told you what you need to know. Now, who would like to play next?"

Otto was shaking his head, annoyed by the vague answer. "I will." He stepped confidently onto the board. "I prefer to use the Tinsley variation."

"Oh," Coach Beppe said with raised eyebrows, taken aback by the response. "Most impressive."

As everyone returned to the black squares, I took a position on Otto's side. A small crowd had gathered to watch the game. As play began, Otto scanned the board like a war general, barking out orders and pacing back and forth behind his pieces.

The game was even for a while. Otto lost three checkers. Coach Beppe lost three. Advances were made, ground was lost. As they played, I tried to watch the game and think about what Coach Beppe had told us. I saw him carefully position his pieces in the middle of the board, always in control of the center. At times he would make moves down the side, but only with support from the middle. As the game progressed, I noticed he rarely attacked unless he had superior numbers: a two v one or a three v two or even, on one complicated series, exchanging three of his own pieces for four of Otto's.

Otto began to wipe beads of sweat off his wide forehead. He held on for a while, but, by the end of the game, the result was the same.

Coach Beppe wiped him off the board.

Everyone got at least one chance to play against our coach. A few players went twice.

No one, me included, got close to winning. Logan lasted the longest time and took the most pieces from Coach Beppe. This surprised all of us, but Logan was still outmatched.

As the temperature cooled and the sun moved lower in the sky, Coach Beppe clapped his hands and announced it was time for dinner.

⚽   ⚽   ⚽

Later that night, just before bed, I went to brush my teeth and ran into Logan in the restroom down the hall. His face was covered in some kind of white paste that was probably a pimple cream. We left the restroom at the same time and began walking back to our rooms.

"Play tough tomorrow," he said, though he wouldn't look me in the eye, and I could hear the disappointment in his voice. "We need to win."

I felt bad for him. It's no fun to sit on the bench. "You've been playing great. I'm sure you'll get in the game."

"Yeah. I guess."

We kept walking, not having much to say. We had been enemies all last season and didn't have a lot in common. Or did we? I realized I knew very little about Logan, except that he and Caden were best friends.

Or at least they had been.

"Hey," I said, wondering if this was a sore subject but thinking he might be able to help cheer Caden up. "Are you and Caden still tight?"

Logan gave me a sideways look. "What? Yeah? Of course."

It didn't seem that way to me. "I just heard . . . I know he's going through a tough time, with the divorce and all."

"Yeah." Logan hesitated. "Did he tell you what my parents said? About him coming over?"

"He said they don't want him around anymore."

Logan stopped walking outside his door. "My parents think he nicked some money off our kitchen table."

I blinked. "What?"

"I told them he would never do that, but a few other things happened." Logan's hand strayed to a cluster of bright red pimples on his arm, and he shuffled his feet. "Listen, don't spread this around, okay? I know he's not himself right now. I've been trying to talk to him but it's hard."

"Yeah," I mumbled. "Okay."

Logan held out a fist. "Anyway, let's take them down tomorrow."

I returned the fist bump and continued down the hall, feeling uneasy about the conversation. If Caden had stolen money from Logan's parents, what else was he capable of?

⚽ ⚽ ⚽

When I reached my room, I found my friends munching down on chocolate cake with loads of sprinkles on top. There was an untouched piece on my bedside table. John waved his hand towards it. "Better grab that, bruv, before one of us does."

Otto licked his fingers. "Mmm. Chocolate cake. My favorite."

"Where'd that come from?" I asked.

"Coach Sam," Eddy said, after he finished chewing. "Room service brought it up and said she ordered a piece for everyone. Wishing us good luck tomorrow."

That was a little strange, I thought, knowing how serious Samantha was about nutrition. But the piece of cake was small, and we had a healthy dinner, and the game wasn't until the morning, and, well, I wasn't the kind of guy who turned down chocolate cake.

I grabbed a plastic fork that room service had brought. As I began to dive in, Otto clutched my hand. "Wait," he said, looking paler than usual. "I don't feel so well."

ENTRY #17

RB Munich

With my hand poised above the delicious-looking slice of chocolate cake, I watched Otto run out of the door and down the hall.

John was holding his stomach. He muttered "Bathroom" and raced out of the room behind Otto. Eddy followed them, leaving me holding my fork in shock.

I debated eating that piece of cake anyway. I really did. It's extremely difficult for me to turn down chocolate cake, even if it just made my friends sick. Maybe it wasn't the cake, after all. Maybe it was something they had eaten for dinner. Or an alien virus I was immune to.

With a sigh, knowing I couldn't take the chance, I set the cake down and went to check on my friends. The entire team seemed to be running to the restroom. As I stood outside the door, I heard an awful chorus of people groaning and vomiting. When Otto finally emerged, he dabbed his mouth with a paper towel and croaked, "Someone poisoned us."

Riley stumbled out of the restroom, followed by Caden, Aron, Brock, and Patrick.

"Whoa," Patrick said, gasping as he leaned against the wall. "Don't. Feel. Good."

Logan ran past us and into the restroom, trying not to vomit on the floor. A door opened down the hall. Coach Beppe emerged, and his mouth slowly dropped. "My goodness. What has happened here?"

When Otto told him, Coach Beppe frowned. "Cake from Samantha?"

"It wasn't Coach Sam," Brock said. "It's the rat who wants us to lose." He cast a suspicious eye around the group, though it's hard to accuse someone who has just thrown up in the bathroom. Some of the team was staying on a different floor, including JoJo, who had a private room.

Then I noticed a few people looking at me. I was the only person besides Coach Beppe who wasn't sick. His eyes narrowed when he noticed me, and I knew what he was thinking.

After everyone had emerged from the restroom, Coach Beppe led us to the lobby and asked the front desk to bring out bottles of water. The sick players took slow sips and began to feel better. Once Coach Beppe was sure we weren't dying, he shepherded us back to bed. The game did not start until noon the next day, and he added another hour to the wake-up call so we could all get plenty of rest.

"If you feel worse tonight," he said by the elevator, "please call my room, and we'll find a doctor. And don't worry, there will be no more mistakes with the wakeup call."

My roommates tossed and turned but eventually went to sleep. As I lay on my back in bed, I wondered if this time the traitor had accomplished his goal and ruined our chance to win the game against RB Munich.

⚽ ⚽ ⚽

The alarm clock rang at 8 a.m.

I jumped out of bed and asked Otto how he felt. He complained of a stomach twinge, but after we had breakfast and took a bus to the RB Munich youth stadium, he claimed he was one hundred percent healthy. Everyone else said the same, which was a huge relief.

The equipment seemed normal as well: uniforms, gloves, cleats. My friends and I kept a sharp eye on everything right until the game started. But all of this worrying was a distraction. I had to put it aside and focus.

The day was humid and cloudy. In the bleachers above the field, I saw twice the number of fans from the previous games. It hit me that we were in the knockout round of the Tournament of Champions. This was a big deal. We had defied the odds and made it out of the group stage. I could already feel more tension in the air. Win, and we advance. Lose, and we go home.

Would our magical run continue?

The whistle blew.

Let's find out.

Right from the start, I was a little awed by RB Munich. Just like the city's public transportation, the team's runs and passes were fast, crisp, and precise. All of their players communicated well and ran off the ball and had an excellent first touch. It was like watching a team of robots built to play soccer instead of a squad made up of human beings that sometimes made mistakes.

Oh boy, I thought as I chased another pass in midfield. *How do we beat this team?*

Minutes after kickoff, a light rain began to fall. The ground was already soft from the previous rains. Now it was turning slick and muddy.

The Germans made a push deep into our half. Unused to facing two strikers, Brock and Riley looked uncertain how to act. Both were forced to mark someone, leaving no room for error.

The striker on the left—his name was Franz—received a pass from the midfield. Without turning, he flicked a one-touch ball to the other striker, Bastian, who fed the ball down the left wing. I noticed the Germans almost never dribbled. They liked to pass as soon as they received the ball.

Sami worked hard to get back but was a step behind the German winger. The cross went in. Franz rose high for a header. Just before he snapped his neck forward, Brock shouldered him aside and headed the ball away.

Eddy gathered the loose ball, slipped past a defender, and took off. I called for the ball in the middle. As his pass came in, I noticed their defensive midfielder closing me down. Remember, they were playing a 3–1–4–2. Their defensive mid, a brown-haired player about my height but much heavier, played right above their three defenders and patrolled a huge portion of the midfield. The name on his jersey was *Riess*. I could see that Otto was right: He was one of their best players, if not *the* best.

I watched him over my shoulder as the pass came in. Instead of trapping the ball, I flicked a one-touch pass to Caden, who was playing Otto's position on the left.

But the pass never arrived. Somehow, Riess anticipated my move and intercepted the ball. He broke upfield, took two dribbles, and sent a long chip down the right wing.

I raced to get back. My mistake had left Eddy out of position, and a player blew by him. I could tell this team loved to use the wings. They did not have true wingers, but their outside midfielders were constantly racing up and down the field.

The cross soared in front of the goal. Bastian chested the ball to Franz, who flicked a ball to the edge of the penalty box. Their attacking midfielder flew in and blasted a shot at the top right corner. JoJo dove high and grazed the ball but couldn't prevent the goal.

1–0.

As the referee set the ball in the center circle, I stood next to John and noticed his eyes were a little wide. "You feeling okay?" I asked, wondering if his stomach still hurt.

"I'm fine. It's just these blokes are *good*."

"So are we," I said, and kicked the ball off to Otto. It was strange to see him on the right, but I had to get used to it. Otto passed to Aron, and our Swiss winger took off down the sideline. When he tried to beat a defender, the German player slide tackled him, recovered the ball, and passed to Riess. I raced to defend but he moved the ball upfield before I arrived, leaving me scrambling.

The next time I got the ball, I fed Patrick on the left. We had not tested their defense on that side. His red hair flying, Patrick made a set of nifty moves and beat his defender. He slipped a pass back to the middle, where Otto usually was, but Caden had made his run closer to the line, and a Munich player stole the ball.

Back and forth it went. Otto was connecting on the right with Aron, but Caden seemed uncomfortable on the left. He and Patrick weren't used to each other. The Germans sensed this and shifted their defense to Aron's side, making it harder for him to get the ball. Again he grew frustrated, not with Otto but with the double-team he kept facing.

Right before halftime, I made a run down the center of the field, where Riess was roaming like a guard dog. I faked a pass to Aron, getting Riess to shift, then slipped the ball past his outstretched leg, hitting John in the middle.

The center back pressed tight against John's back. As the ball came in, John spun around him, taking him by surprise. It was a great move and gave John a chance to shoot from fifteen yards out. He took the shot, and I held my breath as it streaked towards the goal . . .

And clanged off the crossbar and out of bounds.

The referee blew the halftime whistle. John hung his head, knowing he should have made that shot.

"Good try," I said as we ran off the field. "Keep shooting."

At halftime, Coach Beppe substituted Logan for Caden. In response, Caden threw his water bottle on the ground and stalked to the bench, drawing a heavy stare from Coach Beppe.

"What should we do?" Otto asked as the rain picked up.

Coach Beppe opened an umbrella. "They are good, very good. They move the ball quickly and always know where each other are. But remember our games of checkers. Where do you see an advantage to be gained?"

I thought it through and raised a hand. "Their outside mids are good, but they have to be getting tired. They're playing two positions, midfield and winger. Maybe we can take advantage of that."

Coach Beppe smiled in response.

As the second half began, the rain fell even harder. I believe that worked to our advantage. The slick conditions made it harder to trap the ball and make precise passes. The Munich players weren't able to move as efficiently as they liked, but we were scrappy and used to terrible English weather. And I had grown up playing on rough fields.

On Munich's first run into our territory, Franz and Bastian knocked the ball back and forth. They were both true strikers who played high up the field. Brock and Riley had their hands full with them. As Franz received a pass at the edge of the penalty box, Bastian overlapped him, trying to slip away from Riley. But the wet grass caused the pass from Franz to skip too far ahead. Brock stuck a toe in and knocked the ball aside. Bastian recovered it with his back to goal. Forced to turn, he ran straight into Riley, who leveled him with a hard slide tackle.

Brock kicked the loose ball upfield. Otto recovered it and passed to me near the center circle. In the quick transition, I noticed Munich's outside midfielders were caught too far back. I took advantage and sent a risky long ball to Aron, leading him down the wing.

"Let's push!" I yelled as I sprinted forward.

Aron pretended to trap the ball, then kicked it ahead with a beautiful first touch that froze his defender. The center back swung over to cut him off. Aron sent a nifty pass behind his legs to Otto, who had sensed an opportunity and churned upfield as fast as he could run.

Otto took a long shot on goal—or so everyone thought. In fact, he sent a curling pass towards the far side of the goal, hitting Patrick on the fly. Because the Munich defense had shifted to cover Aron, Patrick was open, and he slammed a diving header into the bottom left corner of the goal.

"Luckabucka!" he cried, flipping to his feet and racing towards the sideline.

After a quick celebration, we ran back to our positions. "Nice pass to start that off," Aron said to me in a grudging voice, as if it pained him to admit it. "I want more."

I saluted him. "Aye-aye, Commander Aron."

He looked unsure if I was joking.

"Fifteen minutes!" one of our managers called out.

My observation at halftime had proven true. We had exhausted Munich's outside midfielders and scored a goal in transition. Before we could take advantage again, the Munich coach substituted two brand new outside mids.

Who, I realized after a few minutes of play, were just as good as the first two.

That was disheartening but I didn't have time to dwell on it. The Germans pressed us harder, passing so quickly it made my head spin. JoJo was forced to make save after save. We had to do something to turn this tie game around or they were bound to score again.

Eddy and Sami had been locked down all game, trying to contain Munich's long runs down the wing as well as sliding inside to help defend the two strikers. As the clock wound down, Eddy made a nice tackle and took a risk, trying to cut inside with the ball and create some space.

A midfielder closed him down, forcing Eddy to pass. I raced back to collect the ball and shielded off a defender, trying desperately to think of a way to break them down. Every time we made a run, Riess was in the way.

But we held firm too. Munich's passing was impressive, and their two-forward system was tough to handle, but Riley and Brock played out of their minds, sliding and diving all over the wet grass.

Logan was playing decent in place of Caden. But Logan and I just didn't click that well. When Otto was on the left, he and I could almost read each other's minds.

As the game wore on, I noticed something else. A weakness in their system. Most teams, ours included, used one attacking midfielder (like me) and two other mids that played a little deeper. In Munich's system, they used two attacking midfielders in the center and two on the wings. Only one midfielder—Riess—hung back to help the defense. This worked because Riess was so good and seemed to cover half the field by himself.

But no one was perfect.

He had to be tired, and I hadn't challenged him one on one all game.

Maybe that needed to change.

I waited until the time was right, and we had another counterattack. This time Sami started it off, winning a ball deep in our half and sending it up the line. Otto headed the ball to the center, and I recovered it.

"Let's go!" I said, urging everyone forward.

I ran straight at Riess, causing him to backpedal. Aron surged down the sideline, screaming for the ball. The defense shifted to cover him. Otto was trying to race forward but he was exhausted. Normally Logan would sub in for him, but he was already on the field.

On my left, Patrick was marked by a defender, too tight for a pass. Logan was too far back and in no position to help.

That left me and John. Riess was marking me, and a center back was stuck to John like Velcro.

All game long, I had passed to the wings, wary of dribbling into Riess. This time I kept moving right at him, forcing him back, not giving any other defenders a chance to help out. Eventually he would have to step up and challenge me.

"Here!" Aron cried. "Hit me!"

"Leo!" Patrick shouted on the opposite wing.

I shifted left and reared back, pretending to pass to Patrick.

At last, Riess took the bait. He stepped into my passing lane, and I immediately cut to the right. I saw his eyes widen. He knew I had tricked him.

But Riess was good. Very, very good. Like a cat springing off a wall, he shifted to his other side, just in time to cut me off. On instinct, I rolled the ball back with the bottom of my foot, evading his tackle, and started to push the ball to the right again, to gain a bit of space. But this was a feint too. As Riess lunged, I flicked the ball behind my left leg instead. He tried to spin but I darted behind him, pushed the ball forward, and recovered it a step ahead of him.

That one step was all I needed. With Riess safely behind me, I pushed the ball into a beautiful square of empty wet grass, rain dripping down my face. Ahead of me, John had his back to his defender, waiting for the pass. I gave it to him and surged forward. Using his bulky body to shield his defender, John slipped me a one-touch give-and-go, feeding me the ball at the penalty spot.

The pass was perfect. Now it was just me against the goalie from twelve yards out. I stepped into the shot, not trying to blast it, instead using the side of my foot to slip the ball into the bottom right corner.

ENTRY #18

Advice From an Old Friend

"That's right, bruv!" John crowed, lifting me in the air with one arm as the rest of our team swarmed us to celebrate the goal.

Riess looked away in dejection, the crowd fell silent, and the Munich keeper pounded his glove against the goal post.

We were up 2–1. But the game wasn't over.

Brock roared at us to get back on defense.

And he was right. Here they came again. I was exhausted and had lost my focus during the celebration. When Riess lofted a high pass to Franz, I was caught ball-watching. Without taking a step, Franz flicked a back heel to Bastian, who sent a slick pass down the line. Both Eddy and a Munich midfielder sprinted for the ball.

Eddy arrived a second too late, and the midfielder sent a hard cross into the box. JoJo came out, jumped high, and slapped it away. Franz settled the rebound, pushed off of Brock, and blasted another shot on goal.

Again JoJo saved it.

The referee had her whistle against her lips as the ball rolled through the penalty box, right into the path of Bastian. I caught my breath, feeling sure he would stick the rebound into the back of the net—right as Sami came out of nowhere, slid across the grass like it was a Slip N' Slide, and poked the ball away. It didn't travel very far, but this time, Brock thundered through the crowd of players and crushed the ball upfield.

That was the last play of the game.

The referee blew the whistle, and we were on to the quarterfinals.

⚽ ⚽ ⚽

After the game, the rain slashed down even harder, cutting our celebration short. Thunder rumbled and lightning crackled as we dashed to the locker room and toweled off, whooping and cheering our victory.

Before we left the stadium, Coach Beppe let us know who our next opponent would be: Trevi Internazionale, an Italian team from Rome. They had pulled off a huge upset and beat Real Madrid in the Round of 16.

"Yeah yeah," John said. "I've always wanted to see Italy!"

Coach Beppe patted his belly. "Ah, yes. A most marvelous place."

Before this summer, I'd never thought much about foreign travel. I barely knew anything about Europe, apart from the names of famous teams. But even I knew Italy was the birthplace of pizza and pasta, two of my favorite foods.

I knew about Italian soccer too. Juventus and Inter and AC Milan. Three of the best teams in Serie A—the top Italian League—and in all of Europe. Napoli and Roma were pretty good also.

"That's a lucky break," Otto said. "Real Madrid was the second seed in the tournament. Trevi is the twentieth."

"That's lower than most of the teams we've already beaten," Brock added. "We can smash these punks!"

Coach Beppe raised a finger. Everyone fell silent, eager for some strategic thoughts about our future opponent from our legendary leader. "Now what," he mused as he stroked his chin, "was the name of that restaurant I visited the last time I was in Rome?"

⚽ ⚽ ⚽

We packed up and left for Italy that evening.

I wish I could tell you more about Munich, but we had a short trip, and it rained most of the time. On our way out of the hotel, Coach Beppe told us about the amazing castles, villages, and forests in the German countryside that we didn't have time to visit. I hope to return some day and see more of the sights.

We boarded another sleeper train. The journey would take eleven hours, and I planned to crash most of the way. My plan fell apart as we drove through Austria and I saw some of the most incredible scenery of my life: huge, jagged mountains that went on forever and seemed to reach to outer space. Some of them still had snow on top, even though it was the middle of summer. Rivers and waterfalls spilled down the mountains into wide green valleys with villages and ski resorts. I had never seen anything like it, and I couldn't stop staring out the window.

To be honest, I didn't feel like talking. I should have been in a great mood because of our big win over RB Munich, but I couldn't stop thinking about how Aron and Caden were hurting our team. Putting Caden on the left was a Band-Aid that wouldn't heal the wound. I wasn't sure what the answer was, but if Coach Beppe didn't figure something out, I knew the bad blood between our right-side attackers would eventually cost us.

Even more than that, I was thinking about the latest act of sabotage. Someone had just poisoned our entire team. We were very, very lucky the effects had worn off before the game started.

I had no idea who would do such a terrible thing. But I did know who the most obvious suspect was.

Me.

The phone call canceling the morning alarm had come from my room. And I was the only player who hadn't gotten sick from eating chocolate cake. Even my best friends were starting to look at me funny.

Of course, *I* know I'm not guilty. And *you* know I'm not guilty.

But Coach Beppe and the other players didn't know this.

Was someone targeting not just our team, but me personally?

The thought depressed me, and worried me, and was another reason I spent the first few hours of the train ride staring at the countryside with my headphones on, tuning out the world.

Darkness fell. The mountains became giant shadowy humps outside the window. As the moon rose higher in the sky, I checked the time and saw that it was almost one in the morning. Otto, John, and Eddy were asleep. I should be too. Feeling lonely, I realized it was Saturday night in Middleton and Carlos should be awake. I hadn't talked to him since I left and decided to text him.

> R u there?

His reply came swiftly:

> Yup. Where r u?

> Austria, or maybe Italy by now. I'm on a train in the middle of the night.

> I saw you beat Munich. How did that happen? Did you get Messi to play for you?

Carlos must have been following the results of the tournament on the Internet.

> It was a tough game.

> Of course it was. Like I said before: what did u expect?

I rolled my eyes and told him more about our previous games, our next opponent, the feud between Aron and Caden, and how someone was trying to destroy our team.

> Wait. Why would anyone want the lowest seed in the tournament to lose? It can't be one of the other teams.

> Right. So who is it?

> It's an inside job. OBVI.

> I agree but I can't believe one of my teammates would do that.

> Don't you read mysteries?

> What?

THE ACADEMY III: Tournament of Champions

I read them all the time. The guilty person is always someone you least suspect. That's the way the writers do it. It's like a rule of good mysteries.

> Oh. I didn't know. But this is real life.

Yeah but it's the same thing. No one wants you to think they're guilty. Amirite? You need to figure out who's acting strange. Who wants you to *believe* they're innocent?

> I'm not sure.

Well you need to be. Find out who has something to gain, or a grudge against the team. And there's something else that always happens in mysteries.

> ??

Clues. There's always clues. Did anyone think to find out who paid for that chocolate cake? If it wasn't Samantha, someone had to use a credit card.

> Coach Beppe asked the hotel. Someone used a prepaid VISA card. You can get one of those anywhere.

Smart. So the person trying to wreck your team is no dummy. AND they have some spare loot. You better watch your back and not trust anyone.

> That's not a good way to win soccer games.

> **Neither is eating poisoned cake.**

He had a point. I tried to think about who was acting differently than normal. Caden had not been himself all summer, but he had a good reason for that.

Though what if that reason—his parents' divorce—was also causing him to lash out against his team?

Carlos texted again.

> **I can't solve this thing for you. That's your problem. But do it some other time cuz I'm about to game.**

> Okay.

> **Try not to lose 10–0 to Roma. And remember to bring back lots of swag.**

I rolled my eyes. After Carlos left the chat, I turned off my device and tried to get some sleep.

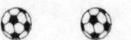

⚽ ⚽ ⚽

By the time we reached the central train station in Rome, I had fallen into a deep sleep and barely remembered disembarking, grabbing my bag, and taking a bus to our hotel. The sun had just risen when we arrived, and I sleepwalked like a zombie to the triple room I was sharing with John and Otto.

Bleary-eyed from the long journey, I fell into bed and slept another two hours.

⚽ ⚽ ⚽

Later in the morning, I joined the team for breakfast in the hotel. It was a small buffet with omelets, breads, juices, and jams. I filled my plate and sat with my friends while Coach Beppe discussed the schedule.

Today was Sunday. Our game with Trevi Internazionale was on Tuesday. That gave us two full days in Rome. This morning, Coach Beppe planned to guide us around the city, followed by a special practice later this evening. That surprised me. Usually, he saved these for the last day. I realized I had come to enjoy his unique practice sessions and was looking forward to this one, however weird and difficult it might be.

As we set out on foot to see the city, I wasn't sure what to expect. I had seen London, Paris, Prague, Amsterdam, and Munich.

Could Rome be that different?

Oh, how little I knew.

So here's the deal. I thought those other cities were old. And they are, compared to Middleton and other towns in the United States.

But Rome is even older.

Like, *way* older.

It was founded in 750 BC. That's almost a thousand years before London. And more than *two* thousand years before the United States. I'm still trying to wrap my head around that.

Rome *feels* that old too. When I'm walking past some of these buildings and statues and monuments, it's like being in a living museum.

Not everything in the city is incredibly old, of course. But a lot of it is. Enough to make me feel like I had stepped into a time machine.

What did we see?

The Vatican and St. Peter's, which is the largest church in the world.

The ruins of some ancient baths where people washed in public. (How bizarre is that?)

An enormous fountain with mythological carvings in the same neighborhood—Trevi—where our next opponents were from. According to legend, if you toss a coin inside the Trevi Fountain, you'll return to Rome one day. I tossed two dimes to double my chances and hoped I returned as a pro.

We saw so many museums, temples, and important buildings I lost count (and didn't really pay attention).

Oh, and Italian restaurants are all over the place. In fact, I began to laugh at how many there were. Unlike other big cities, which have restaurants of all kinds, Italians only seemed interested in Italian food.

This, of course, made Coach Beppe very happy. He stopped at almost every single restaurant we passed to gaze hungrily at the menu. We finally stopped for lunch at a crowded pizzeria where the cooks tossed the dough and made the pizzas right in front of us. It smelled delicious, and when I took my first bite, I thought I had gone to heaven.

No, seriously. I've been eating pizza my entire life. It's my favorite food, along with banana pancakes. I consider myself a pizza expert. I've had all kinds. Thin crust, thick crust, stuffed crust, the works.

But this pizza was on another level.

Off the charts.

In-cre-di-ble.

As we dug in and devoured the pies in minutes, I began to understand Coach Beppe's obsession with Italian food. After the meal, I saw him rubbing his belly and staring at the menu as if he was about to order all over again.

⚽ ⚽ ⚽

By the end of the day, I'd had my fill of sightseeing, but Coach Beppe took us to one last place, called the Forum, which is filled to the brim with Roman ruins and, oddly, wild cats. Don't ask me why. I guess they like it there.

Of all the places we saw in Rome, the Forum felt the oldest. It's just a bunch of ruins—broken columns and pillars and buildings—but the area is enormous, and it seems like the entire ancient city of Rome is still there.

Next to the Forum was the most impressive sight of all: the Roman Coliseum. You've probably heard of it. It's a giant two-thousand-year-old stone arena that's missing a large chunk off the top and can fit 65,000 people inside. It reminded me, as soon as I saw it, of the ancient version of a modern soccer stadium. Imagine that many people pouring into the Coliseum all those centuries ago!

Coach Beppe had arranged for a tour. When the guide saw our coach, he started speaking very fast in Italian and pumping Coach Beppe's hand up and down. I suppose he recognized him.

As we filed inside the Coliseum, I was impressed by the thickness of the walls and the vast number of rows with stadium seating. It even had VIP boxes. I guess some things haven't changed since the beginning of time.

In Roman days, all kinds of events took place in the Coliseum, though most people only know about the gladiators, fierce warriors who were forced to fight to the death against each other and even wild animals like bears and tigers and lions. It's hard to imagine but it really happened. Maybe I won't feel so much pressure during our games from now on. At least I don't have to worry about getting eaten by a tiger.

Once the tour was over, Coach Beppe chatted with the guide again, then asked our team to stay inside the Coliseum while the other tourists moved to the exit.

John stepped forward. "What's up, Coach Bep?"

"You might not know," he said, "that I spent my first three years as an assistant coach at Roma."

I knew that Roma was the most famous professional soccer team in Rome.

"Yeah, that's right," Brock said. "My dad told me that."

"I happen to count the current mayor as one of my friends, and I've arranged for our practice this evening to take place right here in this wonderful historic site."

"Wut?" Riley said. "In the Coliseum?"

"What are we doing?" Patrick asked, and I was just as curious.

One of the managers took out a soccer ball from a backpack and tossed it to Coach Beppe. He trapped it beneath a foot and folded his hands atop his belly. "We're going to re-enact a little history this evening. While the daylight lasts, all of you are going to be gladiators, and battle one on one in the Coliseum."

ENTRY #19

Gladiators

When we had first entered the Coliseum, I noticed right away that it didn't have a floor. Or not much of one. In Roman times, there had been a wood floor covered in sand. Below the floor was a nest of underground tunnels, chambers, and cages for the wild animals. The gladiators waited underground before they fought and were brought up like magic through trap doors that opened right into the Coliseum.

The original floor is gone. Now, when you enter, you can see the mazelike ruins of the underground sections of the Coliseum. There's also a small new floor for tourists to walk on—and that's where our gladiator matches were about to take place.

The managers had brought cones. They set them up to make a "field" about fifty feet long, and goals about two feet wide.

None of us had cleats, but we all had tennis shoes, shorts, and T-shirts. That would have to do. Coach Beppe called out the rules of the tournament: one v one single-elimination, no out of bounds, and no hand balls. The first player with two goals wins the match. Coach Beppe would referee and call fouls.

"Play hard," he said, "but don't get injured." He glanced at a sheet of paper in his hands. I assumed it was a tournament bracket. "First up: Aron and Sami."

As the two players lined up across from each other on the makeshift field, the rest of us stood along the edges, giving them space.

This was very different from the other special sessions and even from our regular practices. Coach Beppe had never run a one v one drill with our team. Why start now? Was it because of the location? Just a fun way to practice our skills in the Coliseum?

Or did he have another reason?

The game started with a drop ball. Sami was quick and sneaky and managed to poke the ball away and run it down. He turned to shoot but Aron shouldered him aside, won the ball, and passed the ball through the cones for the first goal.

Ouch. That was a little too easy.

Coach Beppe collected the ball and rolled it out to Sami. Though he made a heroic effort to beat Aron off the dribble, that isn't Sami's skill set. He tried a stepover move but Aron blocked it and took another shot that just missed.

Sami got smarter and hung back on defense to protect his goal. He put up a better fight, but Aron scored again for the 2–0 win.

The second-team players were in the tournament as well. Even JoJo and the other goalie were playing. At the last minute, Coach Beppe decided to allow the keepers to use their hands to block shots, but they were still at a big disadvantage and both of them lost their first match.

I won my first game 2–0 against a second-team center back. My next match was against Patrick.

"Oh, Leo," he said, cracking his knuckles and rolling his neck in exaggerated circles as we faced off. "I'm gonna give you an Irish knockout."

He shot two arrows into the empty seats right before Coach Beppe dropped the ball. Patrick must have been too focused on his signature move, because I poked the ball between his legs, ran around him, and scored a quick first goal.

"Oh no, bruv!" John cried. "You got an Irish knockout all right!"

As my teammates cheered the nutmeg and roasted Patrick, he ran a hand through his red hair and began speaking really fast. I had no idea what he was saying, but he kept chattering as we battled, spraying nonsense like he did during games.

"Luckabuckawallawonka," he said as he dribbled towards me. "Grittynitty, Leo." He feinted left and went right, a move I'd seen him use to beat plenty of defenders down the sideline. I scrambled to get back and blocked his shot a step before it went through the goal.

"Patrick?" I said as I collected the ball and darted upfield.

He sprinted back to intercept me. "Eh?"

I stopped moving and pointed at the ground. "Your shoe's untied."

He looked down for a split second, long enough for me to push the ball past him and get an angle on goal. I scored again and fell on my back laughing.

Patrick pretended to jump on top of me, caught himself at the last minute, and tweaked my nose. The other players were still howling at my trick as Patrick and I walked off the field with our arms around each other's shoulders.

After that, the games got more intense. Maybe it was our competitive nature, or maybe it was the setting in the Roman Coliseum. Whatever the reason, everyone began acting more like gladiators and taking the little tournament seriously.

Some of the matchups fascinated me. Otto faced off against Riley next. Instead of trying for the drop ball, Otto waited for Riley to settle it, then dove in for the tackle and stole the ball. Before Riley could react, Otto took an early lead with a long shot that squeezed between the cones.

Frustrated, Riley tried to kick the ball around Otto on the next play and outrun him. But the field was too short for that. Otto anticipated his move and hung back. Forced to dribble, Riley tried a spin move near the goal. But Otto put his thick body in the way, won the ball, and took another long shot that bounced twice and rolled between the cones.

Riley snarled and waved a hand in disgust as he stomped off the field.

Next up: Logan and Caden.

I sucked in a breath, wondering why our coach had put them next to each other in the bracket. They were fighting for a midfield position, so maybe Coach Beppe wanted to see who would win a one v one battle.

It was a grudge match from the start. Instead of trying to win the drop ball, Logan caught Caden with a shoulder charge and knocked him to the side.

"So that's how it is?" Caden said to his former best friend as he dove back in and slide tackled him.

Back and forth it went, neither able to gain an advantage. Both players were excellent passers, but they each struggled to break down defenders off the dribble. When Caden finally scored a lucky shot that bounced off Logan's leg, Logan pushed him in the back, causing Coach Beppe to whistle with his fingers.

"Now now, lads. We're all teammates here. Fair play, please."

Logan tied the score with a nifty chip over Caden that rolled slowly between the cones. They fought hard for the final goal, but Caden won the day with a curving long shot that skirted just around Logan's outstretched foot.

As they walked off the field, huffing and puffing, sweating in the warm Italian evening, I noticed Logan glaring at Caden with venom in his eyes. But it was Logan who swallowed his pride and said "good game." Caden kept walking, not bothering to respond or even to straighten his perfect hair as he usually did.

The best matchup in Round Two was Brock against John. Defense versus offense. With a grin, I remembered my own grudge match with Brock last summer. The two of them didn't compete nearly as hard, and there was no blood on the ground when they finished. John won 2–1, mostly because Brock had a terrible shot and no nose for the goal. But he gave John a tough time, and, at the end, they exchanged a tired fist bump full of respect.

Round Three. We had started with twenty-four players, and only six were left: me, Otto, Caden, Aron, Eddy, and John.

"Next up," Coach Beppe said, consulting his mysterious bracket. "Leo and Caden."

Before the drop ball hit the ground, I winked at Caden, trying to throw him off his guard. He didn't fall for the trick, turned his back, and shielded me off.

Caden didn't have good moves with his back to goal. Knowing this, I played him tight, and as soon as he tried to turn, I poked the ball away. After shrugging off his tackle, I took one dribble and scored.

Caden's shoulders slumped as he jogged back. On the next

play, when he tried to dribble past me, I stripped the ball. To be honest, I could have won it right there. But I felt a little bad for him and hooked my shot left. Not really on purpose. But I knew in my heart I had hesitated.

Caden tried a long shot that skipped off the Coliseum floor and into the underground ruins. This time, Coach Beppe decided to restart with a drop ball. I won the drop, danced a bit, feinted to my left, and surged right. Caden was a step too slow, allowing me to get a shot off and win the game.

"Good job," Caden mumbled as he walked off, still not looking me in the eye.

I patted him on the back, worried about his confidence. "You too. I got lucky."

"No, you didn't."

The outcome of the next two games surprised me.

When John and Otto faced off, I expected John to make quick work of Otto. John was fast and strong and had excellent moves. He thrived in tight situations like the Cage. As good as Otto was, his skillset was very different. I doubted he could hang with John 1 v 1.

But Otto was a chameleon. He was clever and could adapt his game to different circumstances. Knowing John had an offensive advantage, Otto hung back and positioned his big body between John and the goal at all times, never letting him dribble past. Time and again, John would streak downfield, only to run into Otto at the goal mouth, unable to squeeze a shot through. Otto even took the lead, scoring from long range on a breakaway an instant before John caught him from behind.

But John was clever too. Realizing Otto was going to

retreat to the goal every time, John scored with a quick chip shot off the drop ball that was too high to block but landed right between the cones and bounced in. Wary of the same maneuver, Otto backed off more slowly next time, not giving John the freedom to take an early shot.

In the end, John won the game by forcing Otto to the goal mouth and pressing, feinting, and dribbling relentlessly until he found a way through. After a lightning-quick stepover, he flicked a ball into the right corner of the goal, just over Otto's leg.

Otto congratulated him and walked off.

In the next game, I expected Aron to beat Eddy quickly. But that didn't happen. Although Aron is a better attacker, no question, Eddy has an excellent blend of offense and defense. He got into his groove, dancing to an unseen beat, his nimble feet evading Aron's powerful lunges. They both scored with impressive mid-range shots, and we all thought Eddy had won the game when he blocked a shot and volleyed a ball all the way across the field at an open goal. It went just wide, and Coach Beppe waved his arms. "No goal."

All of us groaned on the sidelines. No one wanted Aron to win. It would only make him cockier.

The near miss seemed to deflate Eddy. On the next play, he was a step too slow, and Aron smashed a ball through the cones. After applauding Eddy on his effort with all the sincerity of a child promising not to steal another cookie, Aron strutted to the sideline like a peacock as a manager retrieved the ball.

"Only three gladiators remain," Coach Beppe said. "John, Leo, and Aron. Because this is an odd number, and I'm the emperor here, we shall flip a coin to determine who plays next and who receives a bye into the final."

He dug into his pocket and handed all three of us a quarter. On the count of three, we tossed our coins into the failing sunlight, watched them spin lazily in the air, then hovered over them as they landed.

John and Aron produced tails, and my quarter landed on its head.

"Leo has the bye," Coach Beppe said. "He'll play the winner in the championship."

"That's not fair!" Aron said. "Why not a round robin?"

Coach Beppe eyed the sinking sun. "Because we don't have time, and life isn't always fair. So it was with the Roman gladiators, and so it is this evening."

I stood on the sideline and rooted for John with all the other players. I truly thought he would win, and it was a hard-fought match. But with the game tied at one apiece, Aron deflected a hard shot, and the ball ricocheted all the way to half field. Both players raced for the ball. John and Aron were very fast, and they arrived at the same time.

As strong as John is, Aron is taller and heavier. They met with a shoulder charge like two warring rams, and Aron won the battle by a hair, gaining an inch of space he used to pass the ball forward and into the goal.

We all groaned as Aron took a victory lap, wagging a finger in the air.

"No one else took a lap," John grumbled as he walked off. "Take him down, Leo."

Brock gave me an encouraging slap on the back that made me wince. The other players cheered as I ran out and stood opposite Aron in the middle of the field. My opponent locked eyes with me. "Would you like to concede and save your energy for the game against Trevi?"

"Nah. Do you want to lose quickly or slowly?"

Before Aron could respond, Coach Beppe dropped the ball, and we both lunged forward, trying to gain the upper hand.

Our feet collided on the ball. It popped loose and rolled to the side. I got there first, but Aron slide tackled me—hard—and sent the ball flying.

"Easy," Coach Beppe said. "We need our playmaker in one piece."

Aron ran the ball down. I followed and pressed him tight, not wanting to concede a long-range shot. He kicked the ball ahead and ran on to it, but the field was not big enough for him to gain a real advantage. Plus I was almost as fast. I caught up to him, blocked his shot in stride, turned, and took a long dribble upfield. Aron sprinted back, cutting off my angle. I reared back for a right-footed kick anyway, causing Aron to lunge for the block—except I wasn't shooting. At the last moment, I dragged the ball hard to the left. Somehow Aron recovered and, with a grunt, stepped to his right. But I cut back again, this time flicking the ball to my right, turning Aron around. He couldn't react in time, and I had a clear shot on goal.

Easy-peasy.

1–0.

"Oooh," JoJo said. "How's that taste, Aron? A little too much Nando's for ya, bruv?"

With a snarl, Aron stomped back to the center and waited on poised toes for the drop ball. When it came, he charged right through the ball, trying to flatten me. I poked the ball to the side and danced out of the way.

Aron recovered the ball and, nostrils flaring, came at me again. I stood my ground and got into my defensive stance, one foot forward and hips low. Aron twisted and turned but couldn't get past me.

In the periphery of my vision, I saw Coach Beppe watching the game with folded arms.

Growing frustrated, Aron tried to blast a shot right through me. I turned and took it on my hip, wincing at the blow. He came in like a bull for the rebound, but I poked the ball away again.

For long minutes, neither of us could gain the advantage. He was wary of my moves and playing off me, yet staying close enough to make it hard to slip a shot by him and into that small goal.

The sun continued to sink. I kept missing the mark with shots that went a little wide. Aron couldn't beat me off the dribble or get off a clean shot. Sweat was flying off both of our bodies, and I could smell the pizza grease coming off our pores. I wondered if Coach Beppe would call the match if it got dark.

I tried a chip shot and was sure I had Aron beat—right until he leaped high and headed the ball to the side. After running it down, he launched a long shot that I dove for and stopped. I gathered the loose ball near the sideline, right by all the cheering players, and darted towards the corner. Aron followed me, staying between me and the goal, giving me plenty of space. He didn't care if I made a run down the sideline. I didn't have a good shot on goal from the corner.

But that gave me an idea.

I cut back inside to test him, pushing the ball forward with my right foot, taking little dribbles. Aron shifted over, cutting off my angle. I kept going, still to the right, moving the ball closer to the center of the field. Still he moved with me, not too worried.

Then I made my move. I stepped all the way over the ball with my left foot, selling the feint with my body language. Aron shifted again, thinking I was bursting forward, but he went a step too far. Not too far for a normal shot with my right foot, on the right side of my body, which he was now in place to defend.

But I wasn't going that way.

Immediately after my stepover, I whipped my right leg behind my left, striking the ball on my instep with a tough move called the rabona. Mostly it's used as a pass in a tight situation. Players use it to shoot on rare occasions, though it has a high level of difficulty. Since there was no keeper, I went for goal, holding my breath as my behind-the-leg chip shot went around Aron and soared towards the cones. I thought I had missed, but my aim was true, and the ball struck the inside of a cone and bounced into the goal.

ENTRY #20

Trevi Internazionale

As my teammates ran onto the field to congratulate me, Aron shook his head in disbelief and walked slowly towards the ball. He flicked it up with the side of his foot, juggled a few times, and passed it to one of the managers. Then he went to grab a water bottle, took a long drink, and stared at the sky with squinted eyes.

After I freed myself from my teammates, I walked over to grab a water bottle near Aron. "Good game," I said.

He stood there for a moment before answering. "Yeah. You too."

I couldn't tell what he was thinking, but I did hear a respect in his voice that had never been there before—for me or anyone else.

⚽ ⚽ ⚽

After breakfast the next morning, we had a light practice to keep our legs fresh. Our training session was at the Trevi Academy stadium. I wasn't sure why the other teams hadn't let us practice on their home field. Maybe they didn't have the space.

Anyway, the Trevi Academy was an impressive complex with four big fields right in the center of Rome. The main stadium looked as big as the one in Munich. I suppose Italians were just as mad about soccer as the Germans. The Azzurri—that's the nickname for the Italian national team, and it means 'The Blues' because of the color of their jerseys—have won four World Cups. That's tied with Germany for second place.

So, yeah, Italians can play soccer.

After warmups, Coach Beppe gathered us together and patted his belly, probably thinking about lunch. "You've done well so far," he said, holding out a palm towards a bumblebee feasting on clover. The bee ignored him. "You're in the quarterfinals, *sí*? I have not seen much fusilli or bowtie in your game, but that's okay. We are still learning. We'll practice these again and hope for the best. After that, I have one final lesson for you, which I'm pleased to pass on in this world capital of the beautiful dough."

He opened his other hand to reveal an unusual piece of dried pasta. As we drew closer, I realized the pasta was shaped like a star.

"Behold the stelline," Coach Beppe said in the important tone he reserved for his pasta lessons. "An unconventional shape for the chef, as well as the pitch, but that is the point. Not everything is neat and orderly. Sometimes the game of football—like life—is messy and unpredictable. So you must have many cards in your deck, or arrows in your quivers, or, in this case, pasta shapes in your gameplan."

As promised, we spent two hours revisiting all the old lessons. By this time, I knew them by heart. After the bowtie passing drills, Coach Beppe ran a new five v six drill he called the "star drill." The goal of the team with five players—the "star side"—was to complete as many passes as possible in a certain amount of time. This was tough against six players, but he showed us how to move constantly in different patterns and reform our star all over the field, giving the person with the ball as many options as possible. It was an interesting drill, and, while difficult, opened my eyes to some advanced positioning.

After practice, Otto questioned Coach Beppe about Trevi Internazionale. "They play very defensively, right?" Otto said. "Similar to the Italian national team?"

"Yes, yes, this is what I hear."

"What lineup do they use?"

"Often, a 4–3–2–1. Quite defensive, as you say. But remember, their coach might decide to make a change for the game." Coach Beppe shrugged. "We will soon know what he prefers."

⚽ ⚽ ⚽

After a long lunch at a pasta restaurant—Coach Beppe was deliriously happy with his linguine—we walked down the street for gelato, which is an Italian style of ice cream. Gelato is super creamy and has lots of interesting flavors. I tried the salted caramel and loved it.

Before dinner, we had some free time, so I walked around the city with my teammates. Normally we split off into small groups, but for some reason, we walked the streets of Rome in a pack that afternoon. All the locals seemed very stylish, and there were tons of mopeds and motorcycles on the road buzzing around like angry wasps.

Sami had brought a ball. We stopped in a public park to juggle and hang out. Everyone was quiet, not roasting each other like we usually do. The tension in the air made me uncomfortable. One of us, we all knew, was trying to sabotage the team.

Who could we trust?

That was probably why we hadn't split into groups. No one wanted to be seen going off on their own, or with one or two people. Maybe the guilty person wasn't acting alone. Maybe they had a friend or two helping them.

Whoever's trying to hurt the team is already winning, I thought grimly. *They're making us suspicious and tearing the team apart.*

Even worse, I noticed my teammates watching me when they thought I wasn't looking. As if keeping an eye on my actions.

They couldn't really think I wanted to hurt the team, could they?

But I was doing the same thing: following Carlos's advice and trying to see if anyone was acting weird or leaving clues around.

With a shake of my head, annoyed all this suspicious behavior had taken the fun out of the day, I began to wonder if our lack of team chemistry would haunt us on the field tomorrow.

Because if we weren't at our best in the quarterfinals of the Tournament of Champions, I knew we had no chance of winning.

⚽ ⚽ ⚽

The next morning, I woke with a bounce in my step.

Game day.

No matter what else is happening in my life, whether I had

trouble at school or was sad about my mom or just feeling down, waking up with a game to play helps lift my mood. That was true now as well. This was the Tournament of Champions. We were still playing.

Let's go!

After breakfast, we took a bus to the Trevi youth stadium and had a nice long warmup. No missing jerseys or poisoned eggs or suspicious behavior. Maybe the person trying to wreck our team had given up. In the huddle before the game started, I even felt a good vibe from my teammates, and we took the field with confidence.

One negative was that Caden and Otto were starting on their opposite sides again: Caden on the left and Otto on the right. That wasn't our strongest lineup. We had been lucky to beat Germany, with the rainy conditions and a few bounces that went our way. Switching Caden and Otto might have taken them by surprise.

But would it work against Trevi?

As the referee jogged onto the field, I noticed how full the stands were. There had to be over a thousand people up there.

Don't worry about it, Leo. Just play the game.

The whistle blew. We had won the coin toss, so John turned and passed to me. I tried a long, high chip to Patrick that sailed out of bounds.

Brock's loud voice called out behind me. "Shake it off, Yank. Settle down."

His steady confidence helped calm my nerves, and I got into the flow of the game. Trevi's style of play was obvious from the start. They liked their defenders to keep possession and try long passes, especially to their outside midfielders and the lone striker, a tall player named Dante with a mop of curly brown hair.

You know Harry Kane, right? That's the type of player Dante is. Not that powerful or blindingly fast, but very skilled, clever, and a master of positioning. I don't think our defense had ever faced anyone like him. He kept drawing fouls in dangerous positions and making sweet passes through the heart of our defense.

On offense, we couldn't get much going. Trevi kept a lot of players back and clogged the penalty box. They let us cross as much as we wanted, then won the headers with their tall defenders.

Something had to change.

I had to figure out how to break them down.

The Trevi coach must have heard about the Munich game, because every time Caden got the ball, they pressured him quickly and forced him to his left. He just wasn't comfortable on that side. He couldn't get Patrick the ball. As the game went on, Caden's head hung lower and lower.

A Trevi center back intercepted a pass and kicked it upfield. Their midfielder beat Otto to the ball. The next pass went to Dante. He pretended to trap the ball but let it roll through his legs, fooling Brock.

Dante turned and raced downfield, but Riley went into another gear and ran him down. Just before the slide tackle, Dante came to a sudden stop, fooling everyone, and Riley slid all the way past him. It was almost comical.

Eddy raced over, but before he could arrive, Dante took a step to the left and fired a shot from the edge of the box. JoJo leaped to her right and barely made the save.

I let out a breath. This striker was hard to handle.

JoJo rolled the ball out to Sami, who passed to me. The Italians were giving me space in the middle of the field, then closing me down as I moved forward. I tried a quick counterattack and sent a long ball to Aron. My aim was true, and he caught it on the run. He beat his defender by a step and fired a rocket at the goal.

Clang.

His shot bounced off the post and out of bounds. *So close.*

After passing the ball around the back, a Trevi defender tried another long ball to Dante. He almost slipped through again, but this time Brock leveled him with a bone-crushing tackle. As Dante sprawled face down on the grass, Brock gave Otto a quick pass, and we pushed upfield.

Otto fed me a nice ball in the center. I took two dribbles and hit Caden on the left. At last he found Patrick on the wing. This time, instead of crossing, Patrick slipped a ball to me on the ground. I turned as the ball came in, shielding the defender, then used my first touch to flick the ball to my right. I went left, fooling my opponent as I curled around him for the ball.

Green grass ahead. I spotted a hole in their defense for the first time all game. Patrick and Aron sprinted down the wings, calling frantically for the ball. Caden supported me on the left. As a center back rushed to cover me, I saw the best option of all: Eddy racing in from the back, looping inside instead of trailing down the wing. I gave him a square pass on the ground, just outside the box, and he smashed the ball in stride as hard as I've ever seen him kick.

The ball soared towards the top right corner. Their goalie leaped high, his body pointed like a javelin, fingers outstretched . . .

But he couldn't quite reach Eddy's powerful shot.

1–0!

Minutes later, the whistle blew, and we jogged to the sidelines with smiles on our faces. This was our first halftime lead of the tournament.

"Great hit," I told Eddy as we entered the visitors' locker room.

He grinned as the other players congratulated him. Eddy didn't score a lot, so he did a little hip-hop dance as we took a seat on the benches with our water bottles, slapping hands and bumping fists and feeling good about the game.

The day was brutally hot. We were all winded and pouring sweat. A manager handed us damp hand towels to cool our faces. I caught my breath, took a long drink of water, and dabbed my face with the towel.

"Hey," Patrick said, jumping to his feet as Coach Beppe was about to start his halftime speech. Patrick was scratching his cheeks like ants were crawling on them. "What the carabara bean counter?"

All of a sudden, I felt an itching sensation on my face. Cheeks, nose, mouth, forehead.

Everywhere.

It was awful.

I started scratching too. All the other players were doing the same thing. Even the managers and Coach Beppe. People started jumping up from the benches and chairs, bent over double, trying anything to get some relief. It was agony. I put the cold towel to my face, thinking that might help.

"No!" Coach Beppe cried. "The hand towels—I think they are infested!"

ENTRY #21

Sabotage and Dirty Play

I dropped my towel like it was full of hot coals, thinking insects might be crawling on it and biting me. But no bugs landed on the floor, and the itching continued. Now it was on my hands and arms as well as my face. I and everyone else began hopping around the locker room, scratching ourselves and making nonsense sounds like a troop of monkeys to relieve the discomfort.

"No, not infested," Coach Beppe said, shaking white powder out of the towel he was holding. "How do you say this in English? Er, itch . . . itching powder. I believe, yes, this is what is happening. Everyone, quick—wash your hands and face! And don't touch the towels!"

His words cut through our miserable scratching and gave us a ray of hope. We all sprinted to the bathrooms. There weren't enough sinks for everyone, so the players who couldn't find one, me included, turned on a shower and washed our hands and faces with our clothes still on, doing our best to stand to the side and keep our uniforms dry.

Dripping wet, we returned to the benches and noticed the itching wasn't so bad. Within minutes it had gone away entirely, and I let out a huge sigh of relief. That prank had almost ruined our game and caused us to forfeit.

Again.

"Well," Coach Beppe said in a strained voice, as he stood to return to the field. "That was quite a halftime show."

Brock snarled and slammed his fist into a locker. "When I find out who's doing this . . ."

"Uh, Coach?" John said. "I don't feel so well."

When I turned towards my friend, I gasped at what I saw. John's face was so red and swollen it resembled a tomato. His hands were puffed up too.

"Oh my," Coach Beppe said. "Oh my oh my." He turned to one of the managers. "Quick—call the medic!"

I rushed to my friend's side. "Are you okay? Does it hurt?"

John was scratching at his face. "It just itches real bad. And I feel a little sick."

"It's an allergic reaction," Coach Beppe said, as the whole team gathered around John. "Everyone back, please. Let him breathe."

John started to pant and sweat. Coach Beppe brought him a bottle of water, but John eased to the floor and said he wasn't thirsty. He sat with his hands on his hips, breathing heavily, shaking his head back and forth.

Was he going to be okay? As I grew more and more concerned, a medic rushed in, took one look at John, and opened a little black bag. "Yes, this is a reaction," the medic said in a thick Italian accent. He took out a syringe, extracted some medicine from a stoppered bottle, and injected the needle at the end of the syringe into John's arm.

When the medic finished, he noticed the concern on our faces. "He'll be fine. I'll stay and monitor him. You can return to your game."

Coach Beppe looked doubtful. "Are you sure?"

"I'm fine," John croaked. "Feeling better already."

The medic smiled. "Glad to hear it."

"Go play," John said bravely. "Finish the game. And *win*."

One by one, we passed him on the way out, bumping fists and offering words of encouragement. Though relieved he would recover, I knew how much it would hurt him to miss the second half.

And hurt our team as well. Instead of playing a second-team striker, Coach Beppe moved Patrick to the middle and asked Logan to play on the left wing.

"All right," I said, clapping my hands as I ran out with the other players. "We can do this."

"For John," Eddy said.

I nodded. "Yeah. For John."

⚽ ⚽ ⚽

As soon as the whistle blew, the crowd, which had been restless during the first half, got involved in the game. They stood and cheered wildly for the home team as soon as they crossed half field. When I got the ball, I even heard a few boos, which was rare for a youth game.

The Trevi players came at us hard, almost as if they'd been holding back during the first half. I found myself scrambling to help on defense, scrambling to find a pass in midfield, and scrambling to get the ball to my forwards.

Keep it together, Leo. All you have to do is hold on to this lead.

Trevi weren't just playing hard:, they were playing *dirty*. Pulling on jerseys, shoving us in the back, slide tackling harder than they needed to. We had played teams like this before, but in those cases, the dirty play had led to fouls and free kicks. But the Italians were masters at pulling these sneaky tricks when the refs weren't looking. Brock and Riley grew so frustrated I worried they would start a fight.

A Trevi midfielder played a long ball to Dante. He ran it down with Brock on his heels. Dante slipped this way and that, twisting and turning, then took a shot that Riley blocked with a slide tackle, sending the ball across the goal line and out of bounds.

Corner kick.

I raced back to help. Everyone fought for position, tugging on shorts and grabbing arms and jerseys. As the ball came in, I saw one of the Trevi players gripping the back of JoJo's shirt in a crowd of bodies. When she went up to catch the ball, the same player—a short midfielder named Marco—jerked her back, just enough to cause JoJo's fingertips to graze the ball instead of punching it away. Dante was standing in front of the goal. He headed the ball off the crossbar and out of bounds. We were lucky they hadn't scored.

JoJo was furious as she turned to the referee. "Hey! He held my shirt!"

The referee ignored her, and JoJo kept yelling, so much that she got a yellow card and Coach Beppe had to calm her down.

With a snarl, JoJo stomped back to the goal mouth and glared across the field. "Try that again," she said to no one in particular, "and see what happens."

As the game restarted, I tried to rally the offense. But without John in the middle, and three players not in their best positions, we had trouble getting anything going.

And the Italians took advantage. They double-teamed me and Aron, frustrating us, and dared Logan and Caden to dribble past them. Patrick just wasn't a striker and never seemed to be in the right position.

Time was running out. The Trevi coach, knowing they had to score, replaced a defender with another midfielder. I tried to take advantage of their short-handed defense, but our offense was so out of sorts that nothing seemed to work.

The game had started well, and we still had the lead.

We were the better team. I knew this.

But right now, we were being outsmarted and outplayed.

Coach Beppe was right. The Italians were organized bees in a hive, and our team was buzzing around like angry wasps without a plan.

The Italians kept pressing. I finally gathered a loose ball, spun around a midfielder, and surged to my right, into a sliver of space. A tall center back closed me down. I sent a pass with the outside of my foot around a fullback, deep into the corner. Aron ran the ball down just before the corner flag. He whipped a cross to Patrick, who rose high above a defender and smacked a header on goal. I held my breath as the ball soared towards the top left corner . . .

But the Trevi goalie leaped to the side and batted it away.

I sprinted back. The goalie launched the ball over my head, almost to half field, one of the longest throws I had ever seen. A Trevi midfielder headed the ball to Dante, who trapped the ball with his chest and tried a long-range volley that forced JoJo to dive and push the ball across the end line.

Corner kick.

The referee checked his watch. Time was almost up.

"Back!" Brock roared, ordering us into position like an army general.

The Trevi coach barked out orders in Italian. I was guarding a midfielder about my size, trying to stay with him as he scampered around the penalty area. All the Trevi players were in motion, trying to get open and cause confusion. I did not feel good about this. Their complicated movements seemed to have a purpose. What play were they running?

One of their fullbacks took the kick. The ball came in, a short lob to the near post. I saw Dante make a sudden breakaway, slithering away from Brock at the last second. Brock tried to stay with him, but Dante reached the ball first and headed the ball backwards into a crowd of players just in front of the goal. A set play the Italians had obviously designed.

JoJo leaped for the ball, but so did everyone else. The player I was guarding had darted inside. Neither of us would arrive in time. I thought JoJo might reach the ball first, but as she rose to punch it away, I saw a Trevi defender grab her jersey. At the same time, an elbow from another player—Marco again— swung by her face. I didn't think it was intentional, and I wasn't even sure the elbow had hit her, but as a third Trevi player headed the ball into the goal, JoJo fell hard to the ground.

The crowd swelled with glee, elated by the last-second goal to tie the game.

The Trevi players threw up their arms in celebration.

And JoJo writhed on the ground, holding her face with both hands as her legs twitched underneath her.

ENTRY #22

Caught Red-Handed

The whistle blew. I ignored it as I rushed to JoJo's side with my teammates. It was clear she was in agony. She didn't respond to our questions and wouldn't show her face.

As Coach Beppe and a trainer ran out, we gave JoJo some space as the referee did four things: He called a foul on Marco, pulled out a red card, waved off the goal, and pointed to the center circle, signaling the end of the game.

The victory celebration of the Trevi fans turned to groans of dismay. They filed out of the stadium as their players hung their heads and shuffled off the field. We remained where we were, waiting nervously for news about JoJo. We had won our quarterfinal match, but at what cost?

At least JoJo wasn't crying or shrieking in pain. Not that I could imagine her ever crying, no matter how bad she was hurt. Finally, she stood and limped off the field, covering her face with her hands as if hiding a terrible wound. Was her nose broken? Her jaw dislocated? When she reached the sidelines and eased to the bench, we crowded around her, worried the Trevi player's elbow had caused a serious injury.

But when she removed her hands, I didn't see any blood on her face. There wasn't even any bruising.

In fact, I didn't see any marks at all.

"Did anyone see it?" JoJo asked.

Coach Beppe gave her a perplexed look. "See what?"

"The look on that scab's face when he realized they lost the game."

Brock caught on quicker than the rest of us. He guffawed and gave JoJo a disbelieving look. "JoJo—did you *fake* that injury?"

"Wut?" she said crossly. "No, 'course not. Someone pulled my jersey again, and Marco's elbow *did* touch my face. They fouled me then and they fouled me all game. Just, well, maybe not as hard that last time as I let on. Two can play that game, innit? Serves 'em right, the cheaters."

"So nothing is broken?" Coach Beppe asked. "You're okay?"

"Whatcha mean? 'Course I am."

The rest of us looked at her, stunned, and then burst out laughing.

⚽ ⚽ ⚽

When we entered our dressing room, we clapped and cheered and danced. We were headed to the semis!

Coach Beppe gave us a stern lecture on fair play and, although he didn't punish JoJo, he didn't praise what she had done.

I didn't believe in cheating, either, but I *had* seen them pull her shirt and elbow her on the last play, and they *had* played dirty all game.

What was it my dad liked to say?

Live by the sword, die by the sword.

"So who do we play next?" Sami asked. "Barcelona or Juventus? Do you know?"

Those were the other two teams on our half of the bracket. They had played their quarterfinal match at the same time as us.

"I am happy to announce," Coach Beppe said after a long pause, "that we'll be heading to my home country for our semifinal game."

I knew he was from Spain, so I jumped to my feet in excitement. "Deportivo Barcelona? For real?"

Coach Beppe nodded as we cheered the news. Although Deportivo would be an incredibly hard team to beat—they were seeded fourth in the tournament and ranked eighth in Europe—it would be exciting to play in Spain, in the same city where Messi had played for FC Barcelona for most of his legendary career. Deportivo Barcelona was a crosstown rival of Messi's old team, and, at the moment, had the higher-ranked youth team.

Before we left to board the team bus, one of the managers walked swiftly up to Coach Beppe holding a plastic bag. The manager had a grim expression and whispered something into Coach Beppe's ear.

Earlier, while we were celebrating, our managers had gathered our bags to carry them to the bus. I wondered what had happened.

"Wait, everyone," Coach Beppe said in the most serious tone I had ever heard him use. We all stopped moving, confused. "I'm sorry to say," he continued, "that something most grave has been brought to my attention. A team matter that must be addressed right now, as we are all gathered."

"What gives, Coach?" John said. I was relieved to see that John's face and hands had returned to their normal size and color.

Coach Beppe shook the plastic bag he was holding, and something rattled around inside. "This bag contains a canister of itching powder. It was found inside one of your bags."

Brock flew to his feet. "We'll kick 'em off the team right now. Who was it?"

Coach Beppe's face grew sad. He turned slowly and, to my shock, looked right at me. "The bag was Leo's."

ENTRY #23

Camp Nou

I started to shout my innocence but couldn't find my voice. Was this really happening? I blinked, hoping the world would shift and this would all be a joke and everyone in the room would start laughing.

Instead, the room became as silent as an empty church, and everyone stared at me. I glanced at Caden, wondering if he might have framed me, but he looked as shocked as everyone else.

Or was he just pretending?

Coach Beppe's head lowered as if carrying the weight of the world. "Leo, I don't know why you would have done these terrible things. But in light of the previous evidence, I'm sorry to say I have no choice but to remove you from the team."

My heart, already beating faster than normal, started thumping wildly against my chest. "I didn't do it," I managed to whisper.

"Excuse me?"

I said, more loudly this time, "It wasn't me. I swear. I would *never* hurt the team. Someone must have planted that itching powder."

"Two managers saw it sticking out of your bag. I want to believe you but," Coach Beppe gave a helpless shrug, "I feel my hands are tied."

After a long spell of silence—one of the longest, most difficult moments of my life—Brock walked over to stand beside me. He faced Coach Beppe and crossed his arms. "No way Leo would do this. I know this Yank. You *can't* kick him off the team. And if you do, well, I go too."

John stepped forward next. "Make that two of us. I'm with Leo. No chance my bruv did something like that. Like he said, someone planted it."

"Obvious," Otto said. "Much too obvious. You said it was sticking out of Leo's bag? If he was guilty, why would he leave a clue in the open for anyone to find? Whoever did this must know the managers aren't legally allowed to open our bags, so they had to leave the evidence in plain sight. Oh—and I, too, will leave the team if Leo does."

"Yeah," Riley said with a snarl, pointing two thumbs at his chest. "And this bloke."

Eddy put an arm around my shoulders. "Sorry, Coach. I'm with Leo. Plus I've been with him all day, so I *know* he's innocent."

"This isn't right," Caden said, shaking his head in dismay. "It wasn't Leo."

One by one, the rest of my closest friends—nearly the entire first team—stood by my side and vowed to quit the team if I was kicked off. Only Aron remained seated.

Though I was reeling from the accusation, sick to my stomach, I felt a rush of warmth that my friends were risking their futures for me. As we stood there together, waiting to see what Coach Beppe would do, he released a deep, melancholy sigh. "Well," he said, and then hesitated, causing my hands to clench at my sides.

After glancing at the managers, Coach Beppe said, "I'm touched by this show of support. The fact that you all believe so strongly in Leo's character and innocence speaks volumes. And Otto, yes, you make an excellent point. Why would the guilty party leave such an obvious clue?" He sighed heavily again. "Leo, needless to say, you're under suspicion. One more incident like this, and I'm afraid I *will* be forced to suspend you. I'm not sure what to do or think about all of this. But for now . . . you remain a Lewisham Knight."

My friends started to cheer, but I could only sink onto the bench, relieved beyond words and feeling hollow.

⚽   ⚽   ⚽

Our flight to Barcelona was scheduled to leave at nine in the morning. It wasn't that far from Rome—less than a two-hour flight—but there happened to be a sea in the way. Because the overland journey by train or bus was so long—fifteen hours or so—the Lewisham owners had put us on another flight.

Coach Beppe ordered us to bed early. After a late dinner, just before curfew, I took the elevator to the rooftop deck of our hotel and gazed at the night sky, wondering why someone wanted to frame me and destroy our team.

This should have been an amazing time in my life. We were on our way to Barcelona, the city of my dreams, and we had made the semifinals of the Tournament of Champions.

I should have been on top of the world, but I had rarely felt so low.

I wished Samantha, Tig, Carlos, or even my dad was here to help solve the mystery. I knew I could write or call any of them. But what could they do from so far away?

This was on me.

I had to figure out how to keep the team together, keep my mind on soccer, and avoid being framed. If that did happen again, Coach Beppe would have no choice but to send me home.

⚽ ⚽ ⚽

The next morning, as our plane landed in Barcelona, I had to pinch myself to believe it.

I was really here!

This was the city with the legendary soccer team, FC Barcelona, where Messi had trained at the youth academy and played for most of his career. It wasn't just about Messi. All kinds of famous players have played for Barcelona. Ronaldinho, Xavi, Maradona, Iniesta, Suarez, Neymar, the list goes on and on. Barça has won gobs of titles and is probably the most famous club in the world. Maybe the most famous sports team, period.

I mean, everyone knows about Barcelona, right?

The funny thing was, as we left the airport and boarded a bus that would take us to our hotel, I realized that, although I knew plenty about FC Barcelona, I knew almost nothing about the city itself.

It was big, that much I could tell as we drove into the center. Barcelona is right on the coast and has beautiful beaches and mountains. And the weather was nice. Breezy and not too hot, with a touch of sea air.

I couldn't tell you much else. I was excited to be here but troubled by everything that was going on. The city passed me by in a blur of traffic, pedestrians, and buildings. I was gazing out the window with my headphones on, thinking about our next opponent and who had framed me and wondering if Coach Beppe would start Caden again.

⚽ ⚽ ⚽

Our hotel was in a hilly neighborhood called Gràcia. We helped the managers unload the bags from the bus and lugged them to our rooms. I was sharing a triple with John and Otto. The room was modern and comfortable and had cold A/C. As soon as I arrived, I checked my bag to make sure nothing strange was inside.

We met the rest of the team downstairs for a late lunch in the hotel restaurant. Towards the end of the meal, Coach Beppe wiped his mouth, checked his watch, and pushed to his feet. "Everyone please finish up, so we are not late for our appointment. We must leave the hotel in half an hour."

"Um, what appointment?" Brock said. "You haven't told us anything."

"Ah, yes, I suppose it was a little surprise. Pack your boots and dress to play, because right after the tour, we shall use the same facility for our practice."

Brock threw up his hands. "Facility? Tour? What tour?"

"Why, a tour of Camp Nou, of course. The stadium where Barcelona plays. Didn't I tell you? It must have slipped my mind. And then, when it's over, we'll take the field and discuss the pasta and the bees."

⚽ ⚽ ⚽

An hour later, after a short bus ride from our hotel, I stood in the courtyard outside Camp Nou, FC Barcelona's legendary stadium, gazing in awe at the entrance that tens of thousands of fans pour through for home games. The complex was so big it took up a whole city block. I felt dazed as I passed by the statues of former players in the courtyard and walked beneath the giant billboard of current players displayed above the entrance.

The tour was similar to the others we had taken. First, we visited the museum, then walked out to view the stadium. I caught my breath when I saw the endless rows of blue and red seats—Barça's colors—surrounding the most perfect field I had ever seen. I stared at the stadium for the longest time, trying to imagine what it would be like to play in front of ninety thousand people.

Next, we visited the home dressing room, which has a jacuzzi and silhouettes of all the famous players on the lockers. We moved on to the VIP boxes, press room, and gift store. I had not bought a souvenir all summer long, so I used what little savings I had to buy matching Barcelona shirts for me and Carlos. Not the official jerseys, unfortunately, which cost far too much. But these were Barcelona T-shirts that you couldn't buy anywhere else.

Although the tour *was* like the others, it was different in one very important way. Remember the ball signed by Messi I had seen at PSG? And how awed I was?

Well, Messi was all over the place at Camp Nou. Looking out from posters on the wall and from team photos in glass cases. There were jerseys signed by Messi, signed balls, signed cleats, signed socks, signed shorts, signed napkins. I'm kidding about that last one, though I wouldn't be surprised to find some of those too. I drank it all in, barely able to believe

I was walking the same halls as Messi and sitting on the same benches he once used.

At the end of the tour, back in the museum, I found myself staring at one of the countless photos of Messi running to his teammates after scoring a winning goal in a championship game. I thought about what Tig had told me. How leaders on the field—especially Messi—made everyone around them better.

Across the room, I saw Aron admiring a glass trophy case. He was standing by himself as always. Someone needed to talk to him, and I had the feeling I might be the only person he would listen to. I didn't want to do it. Aron would probably just scoff and walk away. But for the good of the team, I forced myself to swallow my pride and walk over to him.

"Hey," I said.

He turned away from the trophy case. "Hey."

"I've been thinking about something."

He smirked and ran a hand across his flat top. "Was that hard for you? Maybe you need to sit down for a while?"

Fair enough. I had asked for that roast. "I've been thinking about how there's no way we can beat a team like Deportivo Barcelona if you and Caden aren't playing your best."

"I am playing my best. I can't control how he plays."

"Yes, you can. You can lay off him and stop being a jerk."

Aron looked stunned that I had spoken to him like that. I wondered if anyone ever had. "Whatever," he said, and waved a hand. "Everyone just needs to get me the ball more. I'm the best player on this team, and—"

There. He had said what he'd been thinking since the day he arrived at the Lewisham Knights training camp.

Except when he cut himself off, just before he looked away, I caught a glimpse of doubt in his eyes.

Doubt because he knew I had just beaten him one v one in Rome.

"Listen," he said, shifting from foot to foot. "You're good, too, Leo. Why don't we pass the ball between us more? We can score a ton the next game."

"What, you think we can beat one of the top U14 teams in the world with two players?"

"No, but—"

"We need *everyone*, Aron. All eleven and our substitutes, too. We've been lucky to get this far. But that luck won't last if we don't change. We need Caden playing at his best, with confidence. And we need *you* to be a team player."

He flung a hand in the air. "Just who do you think you are? You're not the coach. Don't you have some food to poison, or some itching powder to put on some towels?" He glared at me, but when I met his eyes and said nothing, he looked down, knowing he was out of line. I let him stew in the silence. Eventually he looked up and said, in a quieter voice, "Do you know how hard it is to go pro, Leo? I have to get my stats up. Twenty goals a season, at least. I have to get noticed. My dad's a pro. My older brother too. There's so much pressure on me. And Caden . . ." He shook his head and bit his lip.

"He's a good player. Give him a chance. He's going through a lot right now. Did you know his parents just got a divorce?"

Aron shuffled his feet. "No."

"He just needs some confidence. Why don't you try giving him some instead of thinking of yourself all the time?"

With a sneer, Aron turned around and began examining the trophy case.

"I'm sorry you're under pressure," I said to his back. "And I'm not your coach or a scout. But if I was in charge of a pro team and looking for players, I wouldn't want someone that no one wants to play with, no matter how good he is."

⚽ ⚽ ⚽

When the tour was finished, we changed into our cleats. One of the Camp Nou employees let us run through the players' tunnel into the stadium where Barcelona plays their home games. We practiced for ninety minutes on their field, and just being there was one of the best experiences of my life. How had Coach Beppe pulled this off?

We didn't do much. Our legs were still tired from the game. Mostly we ran through our pasta drills and glanced up at the empty seats. I kept thinking about how many times Messi had passed, dribbled, and scored on this same field.

This time, for our trust-building drills, Coach Beppe let us choose our partner, which he had never done before. To everyone's shock, Aron approached Caden.

The rest of us watched them closely. At first, Caden's face twisted up, and he opened his mouth like he was going to fire off a barb. But then, as Aron waited for an answer, Caden looked off to the side and shrugged. "Sure."

I partnered with Eddy, but mostly I watched Caden and Aron. Instead of practicing in silence as they usually did when Coach Beppe forced them together, they began calling for the ball and even congratulating each other on a nice pass.

A few times during practice, Aron walked by me without saying a word. I wasn't sure if he was too proud to admit he was wrong, or whether he would never forgive me for speaking my mind.

As long as he and Caden weren't fighting, I didn't care.

Coach Beppe blew the whistle to signal the end of practice. I caught up with Caden as I walked off the field.

"Nice playing. And thanks for standing up for me yesterday."

He tossed his blond hair to the side. "Yeah. No problem. I know you'd never hurt the team. But who would?"

"No idea," I said as I looked up at the empty seats, wondering if it *could* be Caden after all, angry about his parents' divorce and faking his concern.

⚽ ⚽ ⚽

The sun had almost set as we returned to the bus. I was still glowing from the incredible experience and thrilled that Aron and Caden were getting along, at least for today.

But we still didn't know who was trying to sabotage our team, and our game against Deportivo Barcelona—known as Deportivo, to set them apart from FC Barcelona—was less than three days away.

Would one of these nasty pranks finally cause us to forfeit a game?

Even at full strength, did we stand a chance against the fourth-ranked team in the tournament?

ENTRY #24

The Lesson of the Labyrinth

The next morning, after an early practice, we took a tour of Barcelona.

First, we trekked up the hill in our neighborhood to Park Güell, which has great views of the city and the sea as well as some mind-blowing buildings. Apparently, there was this world-famous architect named Gaudi who lived in Barcelona and designed all kinds of amazing structures, including Park Güell. The stone on the buildings, railings, and pathways seemed to flow and drip and merge with the natural surroundings, almost as if this Gaudi guy had molded everything from clay and painted it, instead of making it out of stone. Strolling through the park felt like I was walking through a dream or a living video game.

Downtown, we saw a lot more of Gaudi's buildings. The best of all was the Sagrada Familia. That's a church you have to see to believe. Imagine a special effects wizard using melting wax to make a fantasy palace at the center of the multiverse. Yeah. Trust me. Go see it.

All in all, Barcelona seemed to have a little bit of everything, almost like a combination of all the other cities I'd seen. It has modern buildings, old buildings, museums and monuments and street markets and fountains and all the other awesome stuff that European cities have. Plus, there are beaches right in the middle of the city where people swim and surf. I imagined it was a great place to live, even if you weren't a soccer star playing for FC Barcelona.

At the end of the day, we took the Metro—yep, Barcelona has one of those too—to a public park on the north side of the city. It was called the Labyrinth Park, which intrigued me, because who doesn't like a good maze or labyrinth? Not only that, but Coach Beppe announced this was the location of our special practice.

Right in the center of the park, just like the name says, is a giant hedge maze you can walk through and explore. In case you didn't know, a hedge maze is a maze with walls made of bushes, which some people call a hedge. The living green walls were so tall I couldn't see over them, and so thick you couldn't see through them. It reminded me of the corn mazes back home that my friends and I like to walk through in the fall.

Coach Beppe gathered us at the entrance to the maze. "Welcome, everyone, to the Labyrinth Park. Technically this is a maze, not a labyrinth. Does anyone know the difference?"

I sure didn't, though I'd never thought about it.

Of course, Otto raised a hand. "A maze is purposefully designed to trick you while you're searching for the exit. You're *supposed* to get lost. A labyrinth, on the other hand, can be twisty and windy, but there's only one path to follow."

"That's correct," Coach Beppe said. "But do you know *why* they are different?"

Otto frowned. "I'm not sure."

"A maze, as you said, is designed to confuse. They can be used as a game or as a layout for a town or a dungeon. Some seaside villages have a mazelike design meant to confuse invaders such as pirates. But a *labyrinth* is something very different. Again, you are right: Every labyrinth should have only one way forward, one path to the exit. However, the purpose of a labyrinth is not to escape, but to find illumination on the journey to the center. A labyrinth is symbolic of our passage through life. The enlightenment and wisdom we gain as we grow older."

I thought a maze sounded much more fun.

Coach Beppe clasped his hands over his belly. "This is the only special practice that will not involve a ball. As I said, this is technically a maze, but we'll treat it as a labyrinth." His lips turned upwards into a small grin. "To win, all you have to do is find the bee along the way and reach the center. I'll be waiting when you do."

And with those mysterious instructions, he began whistling as he strolled into the hedge maze and disappeared from sight.

"Wut?" Riley said. "I don't understand."

Otto stepped onto the dirt path. "Find the bee, finish the maze, win the game. Simple."

"We know Coach Bep loves bees," John said. "He can't mean a real bee, so there must be a little statue of a bee or something we're supposed to find. It can't be that hard. Who's coming?"

I stepped in the lead with John. As we hurried forward, the rest of the team fell in behind us, except for Patrick, who raced by us at a full sprint.

Soon we came to a four-way intersection. John, Eddy, and I decided to go left, but the rest of the players split up. After a short walk, I noticed Sami standing uncertainly in the intersection by himself, with a hand on his chin as if deep in thought. By now, I knew Sami pretty well. He didn't say much, but he was a thinker.

Except this wasn't the time for deep thoughts.

This was a race to the center.

From the outside, the hedge maze hadn't looked too big. But like all good mazes, once you were inside it, you quickly got lost. John and Eddy and I raced down the paths, searching for the hidden bee, taking every twist and turn we could find. It took us ten minutes to find the center of the maze, where we saw Coach Beppe standing in front of a statue on a marble pedestal. I noticed there were multiple ways to reach the center, not just the one we had found.

"Hello," he said. "Do you have the bee?"

The three of us exchanged a glance. "Nope," I said.

"Ah. Well then, what are you doing here?"

A little sheepish, we turned and ran back into the maze. It was fun to explore—I love mazes—but as we investigated every twist and turn we could find, we saw no sign of this hidden bee Coach Beppe must have placed somewhere along the way. The only items we saw were a Coke can someone had dropped on the ground and a wooden alphabet puzzle a child had left on a bench. We peered inside the empty can, shrugged, and put it in the trash. There was no sign of a bee, except for the ones flying around. Surely he didn't expect us to bring back one of those?

Half an hour later, sure we had covered every inch of that maze, we returned to the center and admitted defeat. Most of the team was already there. No one had found anything. Coach Beppe checked his watch. It was getting dark. A few more players filed in, all empty-handed.

Sami was the last to arrive. When he walked into the open space in the center where we all had gathered, he was carrying the little alphabet puzzle, which I found odd. I assumed a child had left the puzzle on a bench and forgotten about it. Shouldn't Sami have left it alone, or returned it to a park official?

But Coach Beppe smiled.

"Of course," Otto said as he smacked his large forehead. "It's not a *bee*. It's a *B*. As in, a letter of the alphabet."

"Right you are," Coach Beppe said, causing me and the other players to groan in dismay. "Well done, Sami. You were the slowest to arrive but have obviously noticed the most along the way. You might all be wondering what this lesson has to do with football. A great deal, you see. On the pitch, you cannot just dribble and run forward like we do when we are little children, chasing the ball in a pack without a second thought. You must learn to look around you. Observe the other players, the condition of the pitch, the formations of the teams, even the direction of the wind and how it might affect the path of the ball. A tiny thing, yes, but it matters. Now!" He clapped his hands. "Enough lecturing from an old man. Your prize, Sami, is already in your hands."

Confused, Sami studied the little puzzle. He ran his hands over the wooden surface, then turned it over and saw something taped to the back. "Two tickets," he said slowly, peeling them off. His eyebrows rose. "To the FA Cup final."

Gasps came from the players, including me. The FA Cup is the oldest professional tournament in England, maybe in the world. Almost any team in England can enter, even local semipro teams with tiny stadiums. The Champions League is more prestigious, but the FA Cup is a very big deal, and I'm sure tickets to the finals are incredibly hard to get.

We all crowded around Sami, jealous, but Brock and Riley looked dumbstruck. They couldn't seem to believe how lucky Sami was, and they were stumbling back and forth, claiming it was their childhood dream to see the FA Cup finals.

"Here," Sami said, shyly handing each of them a ticket. "Take them."

Brock snarled. "Don't tease us like that."

"I'm serious. My dad, well, he takes me every year. I don't need them." He pressed the tickets into their hands. "They're yours."

Stunned, Brock and Riley stared at one another in disbelief, then yanked the tickets out of Sami's hands. As Riley threw his arms in the air and whooped like he had won the lottery, Brock picked Sami up, lifted him high, and roared like a minotaur.

"It seems," Coach Beppe said, "that we have learned more than one lesson along the way."

ENTRY #25

Deportivo Barcelona

The semifinal game on Saturday night arrived before I knew it. The tournament—the entire summer—seemed to be moving at light speed. I didn't want it to end and could hardly believe I was in the dressing room of the Deportivo Youth Academy, pulling on my socks and shin guards and cleats, then running onto the field with my teammates and squinting at the bright lights surrounding the field.

The stands were full. This stadium was even bigger than the Trevi stadium. I started to pull my gaze away from the fans, worried I would get intimidated, then realized I didn't mind at all how many people were watching. In fact, I liked having an audience.

Nervous?

I was born for this.

But something else was bothering me. In Barcelona, my friends and I had worked hard to avoid any further sabotage. We had kept a close eye on our equipment and the other players and locked our hotel doors whenever we stepped out. So far, nothing had happened, but then again, nothing had happened until halftime of the Trevi game.

I was terribly worried the guilty person would try to blame another incident on me. So worried my stomach felt upset.

But I had to put it aside and focus.

Coach Beppe made a single switch to the starting lineup: He returned Caden to his original position in right midfield and moved Otto back to the left. Could Aron and Caden get along? We would see. Everyone else was healthy and ready to play. We were huge underdogs, but that was nothing new.

Yesterday, Coach Beppe (and Otto) had told us a little about the Deportivo players. They liked to play fast and control the ball, similar to the Spanish national team. They had creative midfielders but lacked a powerful striker. On the other hand, nearly all of their players were a scoring threat. Their goals could come from anywhere, even their defenders.

As we gathered on the sideline, forming a huddle before we ran out, Coach Beppe took a drink from the water cooler we kept at the end of the bench. Patrick stepped up to the cooler next. As Patrick poured a paper cup full of water, Coach Beppe began making a funny face. Right before Patrick took a drink, Coach Beppe seized his hand. "No!" he croaked and snatched the paper cup from a stunned Patrick.

After dumping the water on the ground, Coach Beppe bent over and grabbed his belly. His face had gone pale, and beads of sweat popped on his forehead. "Tastes funny . . . got . . . to go . . . to the bathroom!"

The ref gave the signal for the teams to line up. Our managers crowded around Coach Beppe, but he pushed them away and stumbled down the sideline, still holding his belly. "Sorry . . . can't stay . . . good luck!"

And with that, he shuffled towards the dressing room, hunched over as if carrying something heavy. As I and the rest of the team watched him go, shocked and worried, our managers urged us to take the field.

I guess we didn't have a choice. Our tormentor had struck again, and now we had to start the semifinals of the Tournament of Champions without our head coach.

We jogged onto the field. The whistle blew to start the game.

Before I could take another breath, it seemed the Deportivo players had made three passes. Their midfielders came at us in a blur of green and white jerseys, swarming us like mosquitos. They ran all kinds of complicated patterns off the ball, zigzagging and crisscrossing and overlapping. It made me dizzy watching them. Five minutes went by, and our team had barely touched the ball.

Whoa, they were good. How could we possibly keep up?

They played with two center mids, Felipe and Serrano, who made my life miserable. Felipe trapped a ball near midfield and dribbled towards me. Right when I stepped up, he flicked a pass to Serrano, who completed the give-and-go to Felipe as he ran around me.

I scrambled to get back. The ball went down the wing, then back to the center, then off to the side, then over the heads of our defenders. Finally, Riley slid and cleared the ball out of bounds, allowing me to catch my wind.

"C'mon," Brock roared. "Get the ball!"

Except it wasn't that easy. As the game went on, I thought I had never run around so much during a half, and we still had twenty-five minutes to play. It was exhausting chasing their passers around the field.

Deportivo's right fullback took a throw-in. They moved the ball around the midfield and steadily advanced. Their left winger made a run. A sharp ground pass from Felipe split

Brock and Eddy and found the winger cutting inside. He rolled it back to Serrano, who flicked it past Riley to their striker. As I turned to follow the rapid sequence, the striker slipped the ball to another player racing inside, who slammed the ball into the goal before JoJo could move to stop it.

1–0.

And we had barely touched the ball.

We trudged back to our positions. *C'mon, Leo*, I told myself. *Figure something out.*

Sweat dripped off my forehead. I breathed in the smell of fresh grass while I caught my breath. As John kicked off to Otto, and he passed to me, two players rushed to close me down. I could tell they were going to double-team me all game. I barely got a pass off to Caden before the first defender arrived.

Expecting Caden to pass back to Sami, I was surprised when he turned, evading his opponent, and cut upfield.

"Great move!" I called out, sprinting to support him and calling for the ball.

But Caden had other ideas. He chipped a pass into the corner, giving Aron a chance to run onto it. A Deportivo player arrived at the same time, but Aron muscled him off, darted inside, and took a hard left-footed shot.

Bam!

The ball struck the goal post and bounced off. We hadn't scored, but at least we had put them on notice.

We had come to play, too.

As Aron ran back, he gave Caden a thumbs up. At least I didn't have to worry about those two for this game. Now our opponents would have to guard both of our wings just as closely—*if* we could manage to get the ball enough to move forward.

Sami was one of the few players on our team having a good game. He had trouble with strong and fast players, but the Deportivo players were small and quick. Sami was holding his own and making smart passes.

On the other hand, Brock, Riley, and Eddy seemed overwhelmed. They were struggling to follow the complex passing runs. At halftime, the score was still 1–0, but Deportivo had threatened to score many times. Aron's shot was the only one we had attempted all half.

In the dressing room, Coach Beppe managed to shuffle out of the bathroom and talk to us. His face was still pale, and he was sweating hard. "I'm fine, I'm fine," he muttered as we asked about his health. "Just a little bad water." He sat heavily in a chair and took a few seconds to speak. "Leo . . . needs help. No structure . . . in the middle. Sami, Eddy . . ." Coach Beppe pressed his palms together. "Squeeze . . . tighter. Push them . . . to the sides. That's—" He cut off and began waddling towards the bathroom in a half squat. "Okay!" he called over his shoulder. "Must go. Good luck!"

⚽ ⚽ ⚽

The second half started. Coach Beppe was right that I needed help, but unfortunately, he hadn't told me how to get it. Over the next few minutes, Deportivo kept control of the midfield. It felt as if they had an extra player in the center. Every time I got the ball, I had no time to think, no way to be creative.

But Coach Beppe's defensive adjustment was working. Eddy and Sami played much closer to the middle, daring the

Deportivo wingers to cross the ball or take long shots from outside. Brock and Riley were much better at heading the ball than Deportivo's forwards, and JoJo scooped up their long shot attempts from outside the box.

After Brock cleared out another cross, Eddy headed the ball to Otto, who volleyed a beautiful pass to me in the middle. At last, we had a counterattack with good numbers. I pressed forward, dribbling hard until a defender stepped up. I passed to Caden and noticed Sami making a long run down the right wing. I wasn't sure how he had gotten forward so quickly but it was a smart play.

Caden noticed and hit Sami on the run.

Sami took one dribble and kicked the ball ahead to Aron, who was waiting near the edge of the penalty box.

Aron received the pass with his back to the ball. A center back pressed tight against him. As the ball came in, Aron spun, used his size to bump his defender and create space, and took a hard shot, this time with his right foot.

Clang!

Again the ball hit the crossbar. I groaned, but this time, the ball bounced into the center of the penalty box, where John was waiting. As two Deportivo players rushed in, John made a beautiful first touch, pushing the ball to the side, then slammed a shot into the bottom right corner.

Tie game!

I was stunned by the quick goal. John ran in a circle with his palms up, and we rushed him to celebrate. Even Aron joined in, though he was not the one who had scored.

The goal energized us for the next few minutes, but the Deportivo players began playing harder too. The crowd noise increased, and I could feel the intensity of the game in my bones. This was the semifinals of the Tournament of Champions. Neither team was going to roll over. Our pride was on the line. So was next year's season.

For the rest of the second half, we went to war.

Deportivo moved the ball around the midfield. I tried hard but couldn't win it back. Their superior numbers overwhelmed me. Every time I got close to intercepting a pass or closing down a player, the ball floated away, just out of reach. It was like chasing a ghost around the field.

But our defense held tight. With Eddy and Sami pinching towards the middle, Deportivo had trouble getting a clean shot on goal. As the game wore on, I gave up on waiting for the ball in midfield. That wasn't happening. Instead, I hung back to help our defense, playing right in front of Brock and Riley, waiting for an opportunity to counterattack. This made life harder for our opponents. Otto stayed back as well, and we formed good triangles with Eddy and Sami. We even managed to hold some possession, though it was mostly in our half.

Realizing what we were doing, the Deportivo coach made a few substitutions, bringing in more offensive players. They pressed us harder and harder, whipping passes around the center, in the box, and down the wings.

Still we held strong. We had a few counterattack opportunities, and Patrick almost broke free down the wing, but our weakened midfield provided little support.

The minutes ticked by, and the game ended in a 1–1 tie.

As we filed to the bench in exhaustion, I guzzled water and prepared mentally for the two fifteen-minute overtime periods that came next. One of our managers, following instructions from Coach Beppe over the phone, substituted Logan for Otto.

But that was it. No other players came on to relieve us. Felipe and Serrano had run me ragged, and by the end of the first overtime period, sweat was dripping off every inch of my body. I wobbled on my feet as I returned to the bench. Neither team had scored again.

Somehow, someway, I made it through the second overtime period. Felipe missed a last-second header by inches, causing the crowd to groan and our team to collapse on our backs with relief as the ref blew the final overtime whistle.

The game was still tied.

We were going to penalty kicks.

ENTRY #26

Sudden Death

On the sidelines, waiting for the shootout to begin, I wiped sweat from my eyes and tried to block out the noise from the crowd. When I glanced at the Deportivo players, I saw their goalie smiling and slapping his gloves in anticipation. The other players looked just as confident, and their coach was standing with his arms folded, a little smirk on his face.

They want this shootout.

They think they have the advantage, either because of JoJo or because they think they're better shooters than us.

And maybe they did have the advantage. None of the Deportivo players had an especially powerful shot, but they were all very skilled and could place the ball wherever they wanted.

You know the drill: Five players would kick for each team. The team with the most goals wins. From the dressing room, Coach Beppe texted the order of players who would take the penalty kicks.

Patrick, Caden, Leo, Aron, John.

"Knights!" Brock roared, thrusting a fist in the air.

We all joined in with his war cry and gave JoJo some encouraging words. John, our captain, walked out to meet the referee and the Deportivo captain for two coin tosses. The first, which Deportivo won, determined which goal we would use. They chose the home goal, of course, right beneath their loudest fans.

John won the second toss and chose to kick first. Both teams gathered in the center circle, where we would wait as each player took his kick.

Patrick walked out. He talked to himself the entire time, chattering nonsense as usual. The fans waved their hands to distract him. Patrick waved back.

The Deportivo keeper had lanky, tanned arms, a long nose, and thick black curls. He was much taller than JoJo and could almost reach up and touch the crossbar. As he bounced on his toes, hands spread wide, Patrick whooped at the top of his lungs, ran at the ball as hard as he could, and rocketed a shot into the center of the goal. It would have been an easy save for the keeper—except he dove to his left, trying to outguess Patrick.

"Luckabucka!" he cried, jumping high in the air. We celebrated with him and returned to the center circle.

Felipe stepped forward. JoJo walked to the goal and dug in, her mouth set in a grim line. I was impressed by her focus. Unlike Patrick, when Felipe went to kick, he jogged slowly forward, shifted to his right, and, as JoJo dove left, let his foot hover over the ball for a millisecond—right before he scored in the opposite corner.

"It's okay, JoJo!" I yelled. "Get the next one!"

Caden's turn. To be honest, I hadn't expected the coach to pick him. Then again, Caden had excellent placement, and he and John were the only fourteen-year-old attackers in the starting lineup. They had more experience than the rest of us.

Caden reached up and toyed with his floppy blond hair.

His chest heaved once, twice, exhaling deep breaths. Then he ran straight onto the ball, leaned left, and nailed a shot in the upper right corner.

We celebrated again, but the next Deportivo player scored as well.

2–2.

My turn.

As I had watched my teammates kick, I hadn't felt nervous. I wanted them to score, so of course I was nervous in that way, but *I* hadn't felt nervous. Not about my own turn.

That changed as I dribbled the ball alone to the penalty spot, soaking in the crowd and the tense atmosphere, thinking about what would happen if I missed the kick. It wasn't just the Tournament of Champions at stake. Our entire season next year was on the line. Would we play in the Premier League or the second-best division?

I realized this was my first penalty shootout in a real game at the Academy. Despite the thousands of pens I had practiced in my lifetime, and taken in games back home, this was different.

Very different.

"C'mon, Yank!"

The rest of my teammates chimed in, urging me on, and then fell silent so I could concentrate.

I didn't look at the Deportivo goalie as I set the ball on the line and took five steps back. When I did lift my head, I saw him dancing back and forth, slapping his gloves. I swallowed and ran forward, planning to blast the ball in the top right corner, my sweet spot.

And I did. I smacked the ball square on my laces and sent

a bullet screaming towards the goal, relieved I had made good contact and not sent the ball over the top. I was sure I had scored—right until the Deportivo goalie stretched out his body and managed to push my shot to the side.

As Tig had once told me, shooting is a chess match.

And my opponent had just checkmated me.

Dejected, I walked slowly back to my teammates, unable to believe I had choked. They gathered around me, trying to console me. Of course they did. And of course I still felt awful.

I had been nervous before, but now I felt sick.

The next Deportivo player, their number 10, sent a line drive that sizzled into the side netting. JoJo never had a chance.

I put my head in my hands, barely able to watch.

On Aron's march to the penalty spot, he passed by without saying a word, his jaw set and his gaze steady. He placed the ball on the white line, stepped back, and ran forward without hesitation, like he had taken a penalty with the game on the line a hundred times before.

Smack!

Top left corner. Goal. I wanted to hug him.

Our opponents scored as well, making it 4–3 in their favor.

One more goal and they win the game.

John stepped up.

"Good luck," I said, hoping against hope my friend would keep us alive.

"Don't worry, bruv. I got you."

I couldn't see John's face as he placed the ball and moved back, but judging from how long he stood there, I thought he must be studying the situation and trying to outthink his opponent. Or maybe he was playing mind games. The Deportivo goalie grew restless and even flung a hand towards the referee. Finally, John moved forward, taking small steps and approaching straight on the ball. I don't know what he did to make the goalie dive so soon, but when John kicked the ball, his opponent had already guessed left, and John slipped an easy kick into the opposite corner.

John had won his chess match, making it 4–4.

But our opponents had the last kick. If they scored, they won. I thought I had never been so anxious. My missed kick would cause us to lose, I could just feel it. "C'mon, JoJo," I yelled.

But seeing her walk to the goal did not give me confidence. She did not have her usual swagger and cocky snarl. I think the pressure was getting to her. She had failed to make a single save, and the Deportivo players were machines. They hadn't come close to missing.

No wonder they had wanted a penalty shootout.

The referee blew the whistle and stepped back. JoJo hunkered down in the goal. One of the Deportivo center backs strode forward, tall and powerful, and struck a hard shot to the left as JoJo dove in the other direction.

Oh no, I thought, cringing as she guessed the wrong way. My heart skipped a beat and my breath stuck in my throat—right as the shot clanged off the crossbar.

The Deportivo player paused in disbelief.

The crowd went silent.

And our team went wild.

As we whooped and shouted, realizing we had new life, JoJo stood in the goal, frozen—and then slammed her fist on the ground.

"What's wrong?" I asked as she walked back. "We're still in it!"

"No thanks to me. I botched 'em all. Got lucky, shot hit the crossbar."

Knowing we had work to do, our team gathered together, arms linked around each other's shoulders, while the referee consulted the new lists the coaches had given him, determining who would kick first.

You know how this works too, right? Each team gets one kick. If one team makes the shot and the other misses, that's it. Game over. If both players make the shot or both players miss, two new players step up.

This is known as a sudden-death shootout.

And it continues until one team wins.

There was a new coin toss. We won and chose to kick first again.

The referee looked down to announce the player. None of us knew which order Coach Beppe had chosen. I never imagined it would get this far.

"Leo Doyle," the referee said. "You're first."

What? I was picked to lead off, after I shanked the last one?

As my teammates clapped me on the back and said encouraging words, I took a deep breath and walked out. The referee handed me the ball. I set it carefully in the center of the penalty mark as the crowd chanted "Deportivo" over and over.

Their goalie was bouncing back and forth, trying to unnerve me. I looked him in the eye, giving away nothing, and walked slowly backwards.

When I had backed up far enough, I stopped moving and

stared down at the ball. If penalty kicks were a chess match, what move would I make?

The thing was, I wasn't very good at chess. I wasn't Otto. I didn't have a brain like a computer. But what I did have were instincts. Some of my instincts were natural, and some came from all the hard work and training I put in. In a game, whenever I made my best shots or passes or moves, I didn't plan them out in advance. There wasn't time for that. I just reacted to the situation the best I could.

Maybe the Deportivo goalie was playing chess. I didn't know. But I wasn't going to join him. I was going to play *my* game.

I lifted my eyes, and, for some reason, imagined Messi standing in the goal with his arms crossed, waiting for me to kick. And then—I didn't mean to think about this either—my bearded dragon appeared on his head, his back arched, staring at me like a king waiting for his servant to bring him dinner. *Well*, my lizard seemed to say, *what are you waiting for?*

Good question.

I blinked. The two Messis disappeared, leaving the Deportivo keeper dancing in the goal mouth, daring me to shoot.

No more thinking.

I started forward, gaining speed as I ran, watching the goalie as well as the goal, taking in every angle, putting myself in the zone. As I neared the ball, my right foot came back, my left foot planted, and, as my right leg swung down, still unsure where to kick, I saw the keeper lean to his left, ready to spring to the side.

But that was just a feint. At the very last moment, I noticed his body weight shift again and knew he was going to change direction.

In one fluid motion, my foot struck the ball in the sweet spot, sending a line drive to the bottom right corner.

The keeper dove the other way, his long body crashing to the ground as my shot sailed into the side netting on the opposite side of the goal.

"Yank!" Brock roared, and my teammates ran forward, mobbing me after the goal.

I shook a fist in the air, relief pouring through me. "Let's go!!"

The referee calmed us down and herded us back into the center circle as JoJo slowly walked out. When she turned and settled onto the goal line, I couldn't read her expression. I could tell she was focused, even more so than before, but was she nervous? Confident? Scared?

Felipe stepped up. He was probably their best shooter. As he approached the ball, JoJo, unlike most goalkeepers, stood very still, hunched over, her thin arms hanging loose at her sides, staring straight ahead.

What was her plan? Would she pick a side and jump?

Felipe ran forward, not too fast, trying to outthink her. By the time he approached the ball, JoJo still hadn't moved a muscle. Felipe had to choose.

Which way would he go?

I held my breath as Felipe struck the ball hard, aiming for the top left corner. The ball took off from his foot like a guided missile. Finally, JoJo moved, springing to the same side of the goal, taking off from a standing position like a jungle cat leaping for its prey. She hadn't guessed. She had waited for the shot, making it extremely unlikely that she could react quickly enough to make a save.

As JoJo soared through the air, I cringed, thinking she had started too late. But somehow, incredibly, her fingertips reached the ball an inch before it crossed the goal line, and brushed it to the side.

ENTRY #27

Return to Paris

The referee waved his arms—no goal—then blew the whistle and pointed to the center circle.

Game over.

We had won.

I sprinted towards JoJo, followed by the rest of our players, including the managers and substitutes. JoJo was waiting for us with a cocky grin, holding up her palms as if to say, *What's the big deal? Of course I saved that weak shot.*

When we reached her, we danced around her and chanted her name, delirious with excitement.

Patrick shot arrows at the sky.

Brock stood with his feet spread and both fists raised, bellowing our team's name.

And I sank to the ground, hardly able to believe we had won the game and were going to the finals of the Tournament of Champions.

⚽ ⚽ ⚽

In the dressing room, Coach Beppe emerged from the bathroom to congratulate us. He was still pale and sweaty but said he was feeling better.

"Apparently," he said with a happy smile, "my little bees do not need me to win games."

John shook his head. "Nah, Coach Bep. That halftime adjustment was genius."

"How'd you know what to tell us?" Sami asked. "You weren't even watching!"

Coach Beppe waved a hand. "Bah. My managers described the game. I made a simple correction. All of you did the hard work."

As another round of cheers broke out, I found myself imagining what would have happened if some of the starters had drunk that tainted water. I shuddered, realizing how close we had come to losing the game before it even started.

Before we left the stadium, we learned that Paris Saint-Martin had also won their semifinal game. They had beaten Bayern Munich 3–1.

Our opponent in the finals was the top seed in the tournament, one of the best U14 clubs in the world—and a team that had beaten us badly the first time we met.

⚽ ⚽ ⚽

The next morning, Coach Beppe looked even better but was still not ready to travel. He visited a local doctor, who said she couldn't know, without testing the water, what had contaminated it. Coach Beppe's illness wasn't life-threatening, but it had made him pretty sick, leaving us more suspicious of one another than ever.

Who was trying to sabotage us, and what would they try next?

By the evening, Coach Beppe said he felt like himself again, and booked a charter bus to Paris in the morning. The finals were on Sunday afternoon. We had the whole week to rest and prepare.

⚽ ⚽ ⚽

The trip from Barcelona to Paris was very scenic. We saw tall mountains, emerald valleys, gushing rivers, and beautiful villages. Mostly I listened to music, talked to my friends, and thought about the game on Sunday.

That didn't go too well. My mind kept reliving the first game with Paris Saint Martin, dwelling on the size, speed, and skill of their players.

Did we even stand a chance?

We arrived in Paris on a breezy Monday night. From the bus station, we took the Metro to République, then walked to the same hotel we had stayed in the first time. As much as I loved visiting new cities, it felt good to return someplace familiar, especially with the championship game on the horizon. I just wanted to focus on soccer.

On the other hand, I didn't want to think *too* much about the game, or I would worry all the time.

I shared a room with John and Eddy again. Soon after we arrived, needing to stretch our legs after the long journey, we joined the rest of the team on a walk along the canal near the hotel. The light from the cafes and lampposts gleamed on the edges of the dark water. Even on a Monday night, the streets were full of people. We stopped for ice cream and walked a long way, into a new part of the city, talking and laughing and roasting each other, taking our minds off the game.

⚽ ⚽ ⚽

We had practice the next morning. Paris Saint-Martin had agreed to allow us to use one of their academy fields during the week. They had so many fields inside their youth complex—I counted eight—that we never crossed paths with their players while inside the high stone walls of the academy.

Just like in Barcelona, Coach Beppe did not introduce anything new in practice. Instead, after warmups, we ran through the pasta drills and had a light scrimmage for the last hour.

By now, I knew the fusilli patterns so well I could do them with my eyes shut. Run at the cone. Spin around it. Cut left. Spin around that cone. Cut right. Feint one way, go the other. Defenders in place of cones. Passing instead of dribbling. Spin, feint, weave. Run, cut, pass.

Bowtie pasta. Stelline pasta. Triangles and squares and stars.

And then bees.

Bees and bees and bees and bees.

"You are one hive!" Coach Beppe called out after Aron tried to dribble around Riley and failed. Aron had overlooked an easy pass to John, and Riley had made him pay. "You must trust each other. Work as one unit. Achieve more as a team than you can as individuals. Only then can you make the best honey."

He blew the whistle to end the practice. I grinned on my way to the bench, realizing I would miss Coach Beppe and the special practices he had set up for us in each city. Earlier in the day, after breakfast, I'd been disappointed to learn he did not have any more planned.

"You are ready," he said, when Patrick asked if there would be another surprise practice. "Now is the time to remember what we have learned."

We might be ready, I thought, unable to shake the memory of the last game, *but that doesn't mean we'll win on Sunday.*

⚽   ⚽   ⚽

Saturday evening.

Less than twenty-four hours to game time.

I was a bundle of nerves. So was everyone else. We had just learned that, in addition to the fans and scouts who would be in attendance, our game with Paris Saint-Martin would be on TV.

Not ESPN or anything. Just a local station broadcasting the finals. But still— The thought that I would be playing my first game in front of the cameras, for such an important tournament, set my stomach churning like a washing machine.

After dinner, trying to relax, we all decided to take another walk. We ended up at Plaza République, juggling in small groups while some local drummers jammed in a circle. The restaurants and cafes around the plaza were packed. The sun had sunk below the buildings, and I could smell fresh chocolate crepes from a street vendor.

"Yo, Leo," John said, flipping a ball to me in the air. "How 'bout some tricks?"

I did a few around-the-worlds and passed it back. John juggled on his head for a bit and passed to Eddy, who began dancing to the beat of the bongo drums.

Patrick was trying to convince a mime to talk, Otto was studying a statue and stroking his chin, and Sami was helping a tourist who looked lost, speaking in a language I didn't recognize. Brock and Riley and JoJo were arguing about who would win the Premier League next year. I didn't know where Aron, Logan, and Caden had gone.

Coach Beppe had asked us to return by nine. On the way back, Brock and I had to use the restroom, so we walked to the hotel a little faster than everyone else. When we arrived, we took the elevator to our floor and stepped out. Brock's room came first. He opened his door and called out to me over his shoulder.

"Get some sleep, Yank. We need you at your best tomorrow."

"Yeah. You too."

He grunted and entered his room. I continued down the hall. As I approached my own room, I noticed, oddly, that the door wasn't fully shut. Someone had left it cracked open, though I knew for sure I had closed it when I left.

It was too late for housekeeping, and my roommates had left at the same time I did.

My breath caught in my throat.

I reached the door and pushed it open, slowly, careful not to make a sound. When I stepped into the room, I couldn't see the beds yet, so I crept down the short entryway and peered around the corner—where I saw someone in a hooded green sweatshirt with their back to me, wearing gloves and holding a plastic bag by John's bed.

I couldn't tell who it was, but I knew without a shadow of a doubt this was the person trying to sabotage our team.

ENTRY #28

The Mystery Solved

"Hey!" I yelled. "What are you doing?"

The intruder froze in place. I noticed that John's bedspread was pulled down, and the intruder was about to dump something onto John's sheets from the plastic bag he was holding.

As I moved forward, the intruder spun with his or her head down, the hoodie still concealing their face, and ran straight at me. I tried to grab the hoodie, but the intruder slipped out of my grasp and dashed into the hallway. I followed behind, determined not to let them get away.

"Hey!" I shouted again. "Stop!"

The intruder froze again, unsure where to go, then turned and sprinted to the right, towards the elevators. A door opened down the hall in the same direction. Brock stepped out, probably because he heard me shouting.

"Grab them!" I said, flinging a finger at the person fleeing down the hall.

Brock caught on quick. The intruder tried to dart around him, but Brock grabbed them with one arm and lifted them off the ground in one smooth motion.

"Let me go, you big dumb oaf. *Let. Me. Go!*"

The voice was familiar, and I knew exactly who it was.

Brock used his other hand to jerk the hood of the sweatshirt back, revealing Logan's pimply face, his thin lips twisted in rage.

"You!" Brock roared. "I'm gonna smash you!"

"Don't!" I said sharply, causing him to pause. "I don't want you in trouble too."

Two more doors opened. Aron and Caden stepped out, wearing casual shorts and shirts as if ready for bed.

"Huh?" Caden said. "What's going on?"

Brock set Logan down but held him by the arm. "Yeah," Brock said, glaring at him. "What's going on?"

"Nothing!" Logan said. "Let me go. You can't hold me like this."

Brock snarled. "I don't think so. Yank, what happened?"

"I caught him in my room," I said. "Putting something on John's sheet."

Logan tried to yank free from Brock's grasp, but it was like trying to shake off a bear trap.

The elevator opened, and half our team stepped out. Logan went pale as we told the others what was going on.

"What's in the bag?" Brock said to Logan.

"Nothing."

John walked forward, took the plastic bag from him, and peered inside. "It's just some leaves."

"Let me see," Otto said. He turned the bag upside down and shook the contents on the floor. A cluster of bright green leaves with saw-toothed edges fell out. Some of them were still attached to a stem. John started to pick one up, but Otto grabbed his hand. "Those are stinging nettles. They're as awful as poison ivy."

"Traitor!" Riley cried in a strangled voice and rushed straight at Logan with his fists raised.

John intercepted him, wrapping his strong arms around

Riley's wiry form. "Easy, bruv. Take a swing, and you get sent home. Which is exactly what he wants."

"C'mon, everyone," Brock said, pulling Logan down the hall in the opposite direction from my room.

"Where are you going?" I asked, hurrying to keep up.

"To this traitor's room. I'm searching it right now. I bet there's evidence all over it."

"I think we should call Coach Beppe," Otto said, echoing my feelings. "And let him deal with this."

"Oh, don't bother!" Logan snapped. He finally jerked out of Brock's grasp and whirled to face us. "Yeah, it was me. I confess. I tried to ruin this stupid worthless team. But mostly, I tried to ruin Leo." He turned to me and sneered. "I *hate* you. Why didn't you just quit last year? You came here and changed *everything*."

"Um, yeah," John said. "He changed us into winners."

"*You*, maybe. Not *me*." Logan was spitting his words now. "I lost my starting position. My *future*." He balled his fists and took a step towards Caden. "And *you*."

Brock put a hand on Logan's chest, pinning him against the wall. "That's far enough."

"You're the real traitor," Logan said to Caden. "Following along like a little lost sheep. You lost your center midfield spot. How do you think that looks to scouts?"

Caden took a step back, horrified by what he was hearing. "I trusted you. How could you do this to the team?"

"Are you that *stupid*?" Logan said. "So dull and daft you couldn't see what was going on right in front of your nose? Remember last year? I *told* you I wouldn't let him take over the team. You didn't listen. You didn't stand up for yourself or for me. It wasn't my parents who told you to stay away from our house. It was *me*. I didn't want you around anymore. They didn't even know."

Caden took a step back as if slapped. "What?" he said in a whisper.

I was stunned by this revelation, and John shook his head. "Eh, that's cold, bruv. His parents just got a divorce."

JoJo spat her words at Logan. "You're a little worm."

So far, Caden had seemed wounded by Logan's words, unable to process the fact his former best friend was the traitor. But now Caden's eyes sparked with anger, and he spoke through clenched teeth. "We're through. Don't you ever come near me again. Do you hear me? You and me are *through*."

"Aaahhh!" Riley said, squirming out of John's arms and sprinting down the hallway towards Logan, his face twisted in rage. "I'm gonna—"

The elevator door slid open, and Coach Beppe stepped out, causing Riley to jerk to a stop and fall silent, his shoulders heaving.

"What in the world," Coach Beppe said, looking around with a perplexed expression, "is going on?"

We all turned towards Logan, who shrank against the wall.

⚽ ⚽ ⚽

The next morning, Coach Beppe called a team meeting before breakfast. I noticed right away that Logan wasn't present. Coach Beppe informed us that Logan had confessed to everything and was behind all the sabotage attempts. He had swiped the jerseys; canceled the wake-up calls; coated JoJo's gloves with vegetable oil; snuck into the hotel kitchen and put tainted sprinkles on the cake before room service brought it up; poured a colorless chemical in the water cooler; and talked his way into my room last night. Logan had really thrown us off in the bathroom after the chocolate cake disaster, making himself vomit so we would think he'd eaten a slice as well.

I guess Logan was a lot more cunning than any of us realized. The checkers game should've been a clue. Can you believe he planned and researched everything before he left London? In his suitcase, he had brought the itching powder, the sprinkles, the drops to put in the water, a prepaid Visa card from his birthday, a sealed cup full of vegetable oil, and stinging nettle leaves he kept in a plastic baggie. Apparently, the poison "sting" can last a long time if the leaves are preserved. Who knew?

Logan claimed he planned to stop once the coach made him a starter or kicked me off the team, but neither of those things happened. In the very beginning, when Logan took the jerseys, he wanted to plant them in my suitcase. But he almost got caught and had to stash them in a closet.

I shuddered thinking how close I had come to disaster, and I could hardly believe how far Logan had gone. It was both impressive and disturbing. And I was kicking myself for not suspecting him. Carlos had told me to watch out for anyone acting strange or out of character. Throughout the tournament, Logan was being way too nice. I'd been watching out for someone acting meaner or more selfish than usual, but I guess people can fool you in different ways.

It was hard to believe it was over. Logan was off the team and had to stay in the hotel with a manager during the finals. His parents were flying in that night to pick him up.

There would be no more sabotage attempts. No more suspicious glances or mistrust among the team.

To be honest, we would miss Logan on the field. He was our first sub off the bench, could play multiple positions, and, despite everything he had done, had never played poorly in a game on purpose, as far as I could tell.

We would miss him, but I think we were better off. Already I could sense a change in the atmosphere, a stronger bond among the rest of the players, now that the snake in the grass had been caught.

I was still processing how I felt. Although I had never really liked Logan, I never suspected he was capable of *this*. I suppose his pride was so wounded when he lost his starting position that he couldn't accept it. And he felt that Caden, his best friend, had abandoned him and become tight with the first team players.

Unsure who to blame, unable to look in the mirror, Logan had decided I was the villain.

It didn't feel good, to be honest. Even knowing I had done nothing wrong.

With a deep breath, realizing I had to let this go and prepare for the game, I put Logan out of my mind and listened to Coach Beppe's pregame speech. He gave his usual "pasta and bees" pep talk and told us the starting lineup would be the same as the last game.

When he finished, I expected a loud response from our team. Instead, there were quiet nods around the breakfast tables, as if everyone was so focused they had no time for clapping and cheering.

It didn't feel natural, and it made me more than a little uneasy.

⚽ ⚽ ⚽

Game time was 6 p.m.

We arrived at the Paris Saint-Martin youth stadium hours in advance. After a long warmup, we returned to the dressing room, where Brock stood up and told us we *had* to win this game to avoid relegation. Instead of firing us up, pointing this out seemed to make us more nervous than we already were. We knew what we were playing for and didn't need a reminder.

The time came to take the field. We walked into a packed stadium roaring for the home team. A camera crew took our photos. The butterflies in my stomach beat their wings faster and faster.

Coach Beppe had chosen me as the captain for the finals, probably because he felt guilty about the Logan situation. The Bayonets had chosen Javier, and I met my old friend in the center circle as the referee prepared for the coin toss.

Javier ran a hand through his bright green hair. "You surprise me yet again, Leo. No one expected your team to be here."

I shrugged. "Here we are."

"It's very impressive. From the bottom seed to the finals." His top lip curled. "But you remember the last game, *oui*? You do not think you have a chance to beat *us*, do you?"

"You're right," I said. "I don't think we have a chance to beat you."

"Ah, you are wiser than I realized."

"I *know* we do."

Javier chuckled and held out his hand. "Good luck."

"You too," I said, giving him a fist bump. "You're gonna need it."

He won the coin toss and chose to kick off.

I jogged back to my position, wishing I felt as confident as I had sounded.

The head referee ran his eyes over both teams, checked with the linesmen, and blew the whistle to start the game.

ENTRY #29

The Final

Theo, the tall Bayonets striker who reminded me of a young Mbappé, kicked off to his left winger. As the Paris Saint-Martin players worked the ball around, I was reminded all over again how big, fast, and skilled they were. I won't lie, it was a bit intimidating.

Javier got the ball on the right wing and danced with Eddy. Our Bolivian fullback contained him, forcing Javier to pass all the way back to Gaston, the right center back. Instead of taking his time, Gaston tried a quick one-touch long ball to Theo.

Brock pressed him hard, but Theo shielded him off as the French attackers surged forward. Theo slipped a pass to his left winger, who ran past Sami and sent a cross arcing over the penalty area. Javier and Eddy rose to head the ball. I couldn't tell who reached it first, but the ball bounced off and rolled in my direction.

I met one of their midfielders shoulder-to-shoulder. It felt like bumping into a rhinoceros. Neither of us won the duel, and the ball was still loose. Otto and Riley raced over to help, but Javier arrived a step before them and blasted a long-range shot on goal.

JoJo dove high, reaching for the top right corner . . . and just managed to punch the ball away, landing hard on her side.

Sami ran the loose ball down, turned, and slipped a clever

pass to Caden through two defenders. Caden dribbled upfield and led Aron down the wing. A tall, lanky Bayonet defender sprinted neck and neck with Aron to reach the ball, forcing him out of bounds.

For the first ten minutes, we hung with them as the game went back and forth. Neither side gained the upper hand. The pace was sizzling. Every duel was intense.

My eyes kept slipping to the packed stands, wondering if there were scouts and professional coaches in attendance.

Of course there are, Leo. You're in the Big Leagues now.

And your job is to forget about the fans and cameras and play the game.

A pass from a Bayonets defender cut through the midfield. I dove, stretched out my leg, and managed to intercept it. By the time I leaped to my feet, their center mid had raced over to confront me. I feinted left, causing him to lurch, then spun around him, took one dribble, and led Patrick down the sideline.

Somehow, their fullback read my mind and sprinted to the ball as fast as a greyhound, breaking up the play. Wow. I was sure my pass would find its target. Not a single thing would come easy in this game, I realized. Every pass, every dribble, every defensive assignment—they all had to be sharper than usual for us to stand a chance.

We had started well, but as the half wore on, the Bayonets began to have more possession. I ran ragged around the midfield, trying to keep up with them. When we finally got the ball back, Caden left his pass to Aron a little short, allowing Gaston to pick it off. After the play, I glanced at Aron, cringing, waiting for him to explode. But Aron didn't say a word to Caden, instead sprinting back to help.

At least we're playing as a team.

Gaston smashed a pass to Javier, all the way upfield. As the ball dropped out of the sky, Javier backed into Eddy, shielding him off, then flicked the ball to the side and ran around him. It was an amazing first touch. The green-haired winger took off down the sideline with no one guarding him.

Brock raced over, leaving Riley alone in the middle. Otto and I raced to get back, but before we arrived, Javier cut the ball inside to Theo, who spied his left winger on Sami's shoulder. The winger was staying onside, waiting to dart forward. Theo put the ball in the air, a little chip pass on the left side of the goal. The winger rushed into the penalty box. Sami stayed with him but was half a foot shorter. The Bayonet winger soared high, snapped his neck forward to meet the ball, and sent a screaming header to the near side of the goal.

JoJo dove again, this time with her right foot. As quick as she was, the header was perfect, and slipped into the goal.

"It's okay," Coach Beppe called from the sidelines. "Regroup, bees. The game is young."

I felt deflated as JoJo picked the ball out of the net and rolled it to the referee. We had worked so hard, staying right with them, doing much better than the first game.

And still we were losing.

Not only that, but as the half wound down, the Bayonets got even better. Somehow their passes were crisper, their runs faster than ever. We looked like dogs panting in the heat on a hot summer day, and they resembled jungle cats calmly chasing their prey on a breezy evening.

"C'mon, Knights!" Brock roared after a Bayonets shot hit the goalpost and bounced out of bounds. "You have to get back! Stay tough! Play *harder*!"

JoJo took the goal kick, sending the ball to midfield. I ran back to receive it. Their center mid stayed right on top me, so close I smelled his sweat and felt his jersey with my hand. I stepped over the ball one way and then the other, trying to throw him off so I could turn upfield. He didn't bite. I was forced to pass to Sami. He worked the ball to Caden, who found Aron on the wing. Aron tried to dribble past his defender, but the Bayonets player poked the ball off Aron's leg and out of bounds. Aron threw up his hands in frustration, this time at himself.

The Bayonets surged again. Theo received the ball in the middle and ran straight for goal. As Riley stepped up, Theo lifted the ball in the air, a little pass to himself that fooled Riley and left him standing still. As Theo's leg swung back, ready to pound an easy shot into the goal, Brock launched himself on the ground, leg outstretched, desperate to make a play. His toe grazed the ball, just enough to knock it off course and out of bounds.

The ref blew the halftime whistle.

Finally.

Brock stayed on the ground, gazing at the sky and breathing hard. I hurried over, worried he was hurt. "You okay?"

"I'm fine, Yank. Just exhausted."

I offered him a hand. "Great play. You saved that goal."

He grunted and rose to his feet. Together we trudged to the sideline and then the dressing room.

For the first few minutes, we sat in silence, sweat pouring off our bodies, gulping down water. Coach Beppe said nothing different than usual, talking about bees and pasta, claiming we had all the tools we needed to win this game. As I reflected on the first half, trying to figure out how to improve, I realized we had played as a team—truly working together—for the first time in the tournament. In fact, the first half of this game was the best we had played all summer. We were a different team, a much better team, than in the first game, when the Bayonets had destroyed us 5–1.

But an awful realization followed these thoughts.

The Bayonets were still better than us.

The score was only 1–0, but it hadn't really been that close. If we played another half like the first one, no matter how much we played to our potential, our opponents were going to win.

I told the team my thoughts, and Brock snapped a towel in irritation.

"Not helpful, Yank."

Patrick was lying on his back on the wooden floor. "Gotta agree. What kind of wonky advice is that?"

"Leo's right," Otto said quietly. "We cannot beat them like we're playing. Not with these tactics."

Our coach merely watched us with his arms folded. As the silence dragged on, he said mildly, "I have a feeling your captain has more to say."

"Yeah," I said slowly, because I had come to another realization. "I do."

Everyone's head swung towards me.

I stood with a foot on the bench, thinking of my old roommate Robbie, and what had held him back from being a great player. "Like I said, I *don't* think we can beat this team playing the same way. And I don't have any genius formations in mind. But here's what I do think. We have to loosen up. When the game started, we played well, but we were playing *not to lose*. By the end of the half, we were playing not to lose *too badly*." I shook my head. "That's gotta change. That isn't the way to win. Another thing. We've been playing soccer *their* way. The traditional way. Moving and passing and dribbling just like they expect us to. We're being predictable. That's why they're intercepting our passes." I raised my hand. "It's happened to me too. I've been playing like a robot, afraid to take chances. We have to mix things up. Play as a team, sure, but also as individuals."

I expected Coach Beppe to say something about how bees always work together. But he stayed silent. And anyway, that wasn't what I meant.

"We need to use *our* strengths," I said. "Whatever they are. I need to play with passion and be more creative. Otto, you need to use that big brain and think four steps ahead. Aron, it's great that you're being a team player, but now you're playing *too* nice. Boss some people around. Some Bayonets, I mean. Not us. Brock and Riley, be the Terror Twins again. Eddy and Sami, use those sweet moves and make some plays they don't expect. And Patrick?" I slapped a hand to my forehead. "Why haven't I heard a single Luckabucka all game? You're boring me to death out there!"

Silence.

I hesitated, thinking my speech had fallen flat and my teammates were mad at me. But then Patrick leaped to his feet from the floor in one smooth motion, screamed "Luckabucka!" three times at the top of his voice, did a back flip, and ran out of the dressing room, pumping his fists in every direction, shouting nonsense the entire way.

We watched him go, shocked, and then the entire team started laughing.

"Bring it in," Brock said with a growl, gathering everyone together. "Yank's right. Let's flip this game on its head. We might lose 4–0, but it's better than a slow and sure death. Am I right?"

"You'ze right, bruv," John said. "It's on."

Riley started bouncing up and down, JoJo pounded a fist in her glove, Otto gave me a grim nod, and Aron held a fist over his head. "Right," our Swiss winger agreed, and started a team cheer that grew louder and louder.

Energized once again, determined to fight the entire way, we rushed out of the dressing room and onto the field, ready for the second half.

ENTRY #30

The Battle for Paris

Patrick was already on the field, all by himself on our half, waving his arms and pumping himself up. The Bayonet players were giving him funny looks. We joined him and dug in for a fight. Right before the ref blew the whistle, I turned and gave the signal for a trick play Samantha had designed for the last game of the season against the Dragons. We had practiced it with Aron too.

John kicked off to me. I started dribbling to my left, swung to my right, and passed to Caden as Aron cut inside, drawing the defense. Caden sent a lofting ball down the wing, where Aron would normally be. Now there was open space, but as soon as the half had begun, Riley had started sprinting down the sideline. He reached the ball first, deep in the corner, catching the Bayonets off guard just as he had the Dragons.

Otto, Caden, and I were all racing forward, overloading the attack. Our opponents scrambled to get back. Riley sent a ground pass behind John and Aron, right into my path. As a defender closed in, I drew my leg back to shoot . . .

And stepped over the ball, fooling the defense once again, opening up a lane for Otto.

Bam!

My friend's strong right-footed shot hit the goalpost and soared over the top. A near miss that had the Bayonets reeling. We might not have scored, but our aggressive move had set a new tone for the game.

Could we keep it up?

Gaston took the goal kick. Their midfielders worked the ball around as we fought to contain them. Eventually they found Theo at the top of the penalty box. As he side-stepped Brock and prepared to unleash a left-footed bullet, Riley raced in, launched his body through the air, and slide tackled Theo with both feet. Riley got the ball first, but he also took out Theo and a clump of grass before landing hard on his side.

I thought Riley might have hurt himself, but he jumped to his feet, shook a fist in the air, mumbled something in Manchester slang, and gave a Bayonet player standing near the play a shove for good measure. I cringed as the referee reached into his pocket, about to whip out a card, but he thought better of it and let the play continue.

As Theo struggled to his feet, I saw Brock and Riley slap hands and glare downfield, as if to say, *You better think twice about coming back here.*

Caden recovered the ball. He completed a smooth give-and-go with Aron, sprinting down the wing and then launching a wicked cross to Patrick. As the ball screamed in, Patrick leaped higher than ever, soaring over a much taller defender. His head snapped down to meet the ball at the perfect angle—*crack!*—and the ball took off towards the far corner of the goal.

But the Bayonets goalie had read the play. He scrambled back and timed his save perfectly, caught the ball as he fell, bounced up, and threw a long ball to midfield. The pass was headed for their center midfielder, who was cutting to his right to take the ball over his shoulder, aiming for a quick pass to Javier. It was a great play—except they had done the same thing three times already. This time, I anticipated the throw and ran to cover it. As soon as their center mid trapped the ball, I poked it away, then ran around him on the other side.

Quick as a thunderclap, we had a counterattack.

I kept my head up as I dribbled, observing the field like a war general. We had even numbers. Otto on my left, Caden on my right, and all my forwards in position. I surged upfield, forcing a defender to commit. Once he did, I passed to Caden and whirled around my defender.

Caden gave it right back. I received the ball as Gaston stepped up. This time I faked a pass to Otto and spun around Gaston, fooling him completely with my Maradona. I had made both of these spin moves on instinct, but I realized, in the back of my mind, they were part of our fusilli drills.

The other center back closed me off. I passed to Otto and darted to my left. Otto fed me another one-touch pass, still working the fusilli drill, leading me deep into enemy territory. I dribbled once, into a pocket of space near the endline, right inside the penalty box on the left side of the goal.

But I had nowhere to go. Two defenders had closed me down, and I was facing the endline. Reacting quickly, before the defense could get set, I spun again, yet another fusilli move, and noticed Patrick making a run behind me. Halfway through the spin, I improvised and passed to Patrick with a back heel, splitting both defenders.

Somehow the risky no-look pass found its target. Patrick hit the ball in stride, sending a missile past the goalie at point blank range. The poor guy never had a chance.

Goal!

We celebrated wildly. Some of the fans even cheered for us. But the loudest cry of all came from Coach Beppe, who threw his hands in the air, leaned back, and gave an exultant shout. "Ah, *sí*, the fusilli! At last, at last, at last!!!!"

As he began dancing a little jig on the sideline, kicking up his heels and swinging his arms back and forth, I caught up with Patrick. He was spinning in place, shooting arrows at the crowd. "Okay," I said with a laugh. "Not too much. We don't want a card."

He shot one more arrow, leaped high, and landed low with his arms and fingers spread, a pose I'd never seen before. "Aikiki!!" he cried before running back to his position.

The Bayonets looked stunned we had tied the game. We kept up our chatter as play resumed, trying to knock them out of their comfort zone, tackling them hard and never giving up on a ball.

But they were the number one seed for a reason.

As the half went on, they took control of the game, whipping passes back and forth, using their speed on long runs down the wing, overloading the midfield, bullying us off the ball with their size and strength.

"Stay the course, Knights," Coach Beppe yelled from the bench. "You have everything you need."

What kind of mysterious advice is that? I thought as I chased another pass, a step behind the play. Just like in the first game, the Bayonets were using their 4–2–3–1 formation to pack the midfield. As soon as we closed in to defend them, they released their speedy wingers down the sidelines.

Just before I reached their center mid, he found Javier streaking towards the corner flag, a step quicker than Eddy.

Javier started to cross the ball when Brock flattened him, hardly bothering with a play on the ball.

The whistle blew—and a yellow card came out.

Brock didn't care. He had made his point again, trying to intimidate the other team. He ran back and directed traffic as we all hustled to get in place to defend the dangerous free kick.

Javier pushed slowly to his feet, glared at Brock, set the ball down, and backed up to kick. JoJo set up a wall. I was in the penalty box, trying to cover someone six inches taller.

The ball came in, bending and dipping towards the goal. Aron leaped up and headed it out. The ball soared to the edge of the box and bounced. Riley tried to volley it but barely grazed the ball. It bounced again. Somehow Gaston toe-poked the ball through a crowd of players, and it ended up at Theo's feet. Sami stepped up, but Theo made a slick move to his left, a quick one-two that left Sami staring at the grass.

JoJo rushed out, trying to cut off Theo's angle, but he shifted his body to the right and slipped a pass around her, into the side netting.

I groaned and put my hands against my head.

"That was a dumb foul," Javier said as he ran by Brock. "But thank you for the goal."

As Brock's face turned red, I hurried to grab his arm and steer him away. "He's trying to get a reaction," I said. "If you get another card, we lose for sure."

Brock grunted, shook off my arm, and stalked back to his position.

The referee set the ball in the center circle. Sweat dripped off my forehead and stung my eyes. My jersey was soaking wet. The cheers of the home crowd rang in my ears. I worked hard to catch my breath, ignoring the packed stadium and the camera crew and focusing on the game clock and scoreboard.

Twenty minutes to go.

Down 2–1.

Never had the mountain seemed so high.

"Get me the ball," Aron said as he jogged past.

I nodded to conserve my energy, glad he was so confident, and joined John at the center circle. He kicked off to me. I flicked a pass to Caden and pushed forward, but Caden sent the ball back to Sami, causing Aron to throw up his hands in frustration. I showed him my palms, asking for patience.

When the ball came to Sami, he fooled everyone and one-touched the ball forward, past his opponent, then ran on to it. Sami, at a size and speed disadvantage against the Bayonets, had played conservative all game. But his clever move had gained him some space and opened up the field.

A Bayonet midfielder, forced to close Sami down, left Caden and ran towards the ball. Sami curved a pass around him and hit Caden on the run. Caden stepped over the ball, fooling another defender, and sent a pass to me behind his legs. Slick move. I spied John coming back to help and rewarded him a pass. He sent the ball to Otto, who immediately found Eddy on the overlap.

The Bayonets were on their heels, trying to follow our quick passes and dizzying movements off the ball. Patrick cut inside. Eddy fed him the ball, and Patrick used the bottom of his foot to roll the ball to me without looking. In the corner of my eye, I noticed Aron streaking towards the goal. With another first touch, I chipped the ball to the back side of the goal, trying to reach him.

My quick pass to avoid the defense wasn't perfect, but at least it would allow Aron to head the ball on goal. He leaped high, ready to challenge the goalie. Everyone in the stadium, me included, thought he would try to score.

But this time, Aron did something different. Sami, who had started the whole play, was running in behind him. Somehow Aron knew this. Instead of heading the ball, Aron let it fall to his chest, directing yet another one-touch pass to his left—right into Sami's path. Sami's stubby leg swung back, and he smacked the ball in stride, aiming for the bottom left corner. I caught my breath as the goalie dove, stretched out to his full length, hit the ground hard . . .

And just missed the ball, which skidded into the back netting.

"My bees!" Coach Beppe cried from the sidelines as we tied the game, waggling his fingers back and forth in the air as he hopped up and down. "My little bees have done it!"

I knew what he meant. Nearly the whole team had contributed to that goal, whipping passes around the defense in perfect harmony before they could get set. We all gathered around Sami, congratulating his magical run that ended with a goal, then jogged back to our positions, not wanting to expend too much energy on a celebration. We still had fifteen minutes to go, and I could tell that every single one of my teammates was as exhausted as I was.

During the break in action, the Paris coach made four substitutions, three of them in midfield. My heart sank. From experience, I knew their substitutes were almost as good as their starters. And they all had fresh legs.

I glanced at our bench. Coach Beppe beamed a smile and didn't make a single change.

With a deep breath, I prepared for the assault I knew was coming. The Bayonet players didn't look at all disheartened by our goal.

Instead, they looked angry. As if we had poked a nest of hornets about to chase a bunch of puny little bees around a field.

Play restarted.

Theo whipped a pass to Javier as their entire team pushed forward.

Here they come.

I braced for the attack, staying on my toes, running neck and neck with their new center mid. He received a pass and tried to surge ahead but I dug deep and poked the ball away. There was a scramble for possession. Otto came up with the ball, feinted left, pulled back, and passed to me. My teammates could have given in to their exhaustion, but instead they kept moving off the ball, forming triangles and squares, giving me options. Somehow, for the next few minutes, we pushed ourselves past our limits and managed to keep the ball as much as the Bayonets.

But that didn't last. Our opponents were furious and pressing hard. Theo slammed a shot off the crossbar. JoJo saved a left-footed rocket by Javier. They came at us again and again, moving the ball through the middle, finding Theo on breakaways, sending long balls down the wings. Riley fouled Theo hard again on their next trip downfield, earning a yellow card. He and Brock had been everywhere, sliding for every tackle, winning every header.

But now they were both sitting on a yellow.

Theo lined up for the free kick. He curled the ball around

the wall, and I caught my breath as it soared towards the top right corner. JoJo was caught on the opposite side of the goal. Just before the shot landed in the net, Eddy dove to the side, sacrificing his body, barely managing to head the ball away before he crashed into the goalpost and fell to the ground.

Brock and I hustled over to help him up. A little dazed, Eddy stood and scrambled back to cover Javier.

Their attacks came in wave after wave. We were surviving on sheer guts. I had never been so exhausted. As Sami blasted the ball out of bounds to give us a breather, I stood with my hands on my hips, chest heaving, and had a sudden troubling thought.

The game was still tied, and we couldn't win in overtime. No way. We were just too exhausted. I could see more Bayonets warming up on the sidelines, passing the ball back and forth with confident expressions, knowing they were about to come in and overwhelm us.

I looked at the game clock.

Regulation had ended. We had two minutes of extra time. The next one hundred and twenty seconds would make or break us. I searched deep inside for energy but found an empty well instead. We were all so fatigued I didn't think we could possibly score in that short window of time.

But we had to try.

It was now or never.

The ball came in. As their right midfielder waited to receive the pass, Otto sprinted forward, sliding on his side across the field, and poked the ball to Eddy. He sent the ball to me. As I ran to meet the pass, I noticed Otto getting up very slowly, wobbling on his feet. Normally Logan would have subbed for him by now.

With a grimace, I realized Otto was done for the game.

Someone was pressing hard against my back. I sent my first touch to the side, trying to gain space. My defender stayed with me, but I cut hard upfield, keeping my shoulder between us, just managing to turn the corner. With a burst of speed—I don't even know where it came from—I surged ahead and crossed midfield.

John came back to help. "Here, Leo!"

I gave him the ball and pushed forward, dragging a defender with me. John faked a return pass and slipped the ball to Patrick, who was cutting inside. A defender slide tackled him, sending the ball flying in the other direction. Oh no. All my energy left my body. I thought the Bayonets would regain possession, and that would be the last play of regulation, but then Otto ran out of nowhere to recover the ball!

Breathing heavily, Otto put a toe on the ball, sent a long pass to Aron, and then fell to the ground holding his calf, no doubt suffering from a cramp. Now he was done for sure. The referee signaled for us to play on. He wasn't stopping the game in the last few moments.

Aron tried to break free, but his defender was too good. He forced Aron to pass back to Caden, and I glanced at the clock again. Twenty seconds left. We had the ball but were going nowhere, stuck in midfield.

The Bayonets defense had settled in, knowing this was the last gasp. They had numbers, too, since Otto was out. I sucked in a deep breath and pressed forward. Caden skipped a pass to me on the ground. A defender stepped up, and I started to make a one-touch pass back to Caden. We had been doing this all half. My defender stuck a leg out, trying to intercept it, but I used a Cruyff turn to whip around in the other direction, leaving him in the dust.

I flicked a pass to John and ran ahead. "Here!"

He slipped the ball to me as I raced past him near the edge of the penalty box. Both center backs, Gaston and another giant, stood between me and the goal. Patrick and Aron were on the wings but marked by defenders. John was still behind me. Caden was too far back to help.

I hesitated, deciding between Aron and Patrick, then pushed the ball forward, deeper into the box. I wasn't sure what I was doing, and I meant to pass the ball. I really did. But when both center backs stepped up to cut me off, I noticed something. Neither of them was coming straight at me. They were playing a little to each side, not wanting to commit, each of them probably thinking the other would close me down. It wasn't much. Just a tiny little window.

Surely, they must be thinking, *this little guy would never try beating us both.*

But it was too late. I had made up my mind. Pasta and bees had gotten us this far, but sometimes, you have to be creative and follow your instincts. As the center backs closed in, I poked the ball forward, a little pass to myself right between those two trees. The ball barely got through, and I saw the surprise on their faces. As I followed the ball, they tried to close me off, slamming together like heavy double doors, trying to make a Leo sandwich.

But I slithered through, bouncing off their broad shoulders, slipping through their sweat-soaked shirts, willing myself forward. I stumbled and almost fell but managed to find my balance. Now I was at the penalty spot, right in front of the goal.

The only problem was the final defender—the goalie—who was racing out for the ball.

It was going to be close. Too close. My heart sank as I realized I wouldn't reach the ball in time to dribble around him. I planned to chip it over him, but as I stepped forward, the goalie dove, sliding forward with his hands up, reading my mind and making the smart play. A chip shot wouldn't work. He was about to pounce on the ball, and I had nowhere to go.

But someone else might. On my right, I spied two players closing in, Aron and a defender racing alongside him. Without thinking, I flicked the ball forward, just over the goalie's outstretched leg, a diagonal little chip pass that, if the stars aligned, might catch Aron in stride.

As soon as the ball left my foot, I turned and saw the fullback who had shut Aron down all game running a step ahead of him. The defender was going to reach the ball first and head it away. *Oh no*, I thought—right as Aron grunted and launched his body into the air. With a superhuman effort, he reached the ball a millisecond before his defender and somehow, impossibly, got a head on my flick pass that was hanging in the air.

The Bayonets goalie could only turn on the ground, helpless, and watch Aron's header soar through the air and into the goal.

ENTRY #31

The Last Challenge

The final whistle blew.

I sank to my knees, too exhausted to move, stunned we had pulled off the impossible and won the game.

In front of me, Aron was standing by the goal with his arms raised, his head tilted towards the sky. When he turned, I noticed that, instead of his usual smug expression, he looked happy and almost . . . relieved.

John's strong arms lifted me up from behind. "Bruv, did you really now? Bossed two defenders and pulled off that ridiculous flick?"

"Knights!" Brock roared, wrapping his arms around me and John.

Aron ran over, and Patrick slammed into all four of us, bowling us to the ground. More players jumped on top, a giant pile of laughter and wild cheering that grew and grew and grew. Eventually, we separated and made our way to the sideline while the Paris Saint-Martin players left the field. Some covered their faces with their shirts; others stumbled forward in a state of shock and disbelief. Javier was lying on his back on the grass, chest heaving, staring at the bright lights.

I walked towards him and offered a hand. "Good game," I said, helping him to his feet.

"You too," he mumbled. "You earned that win."

"Thanks."

He ran a hand through his bright green hair. "We'll meet again, Leo. Of this, I am sure."

I fist-bumped him. "No doubt."

My teammates were dancing around Coach Beppe, shouting and clapping. As I joined them, he held up a finger, stroking his chin with a grave expression. We all quieted, wondering what final words of wisdom he would impart to the team after such a great victory.

"Now where is the best place," he mused as if asking himself a question, "for a celebratory dinner?"

⚽ ⚽ ⚽

Right after the game, before we left the field, the organizers of the tournament handed out awards. JoJo was voted Best Goalkeeper, Brock and Riley were named Co-defensive Players of the Tournament, and Theo won the Golden Boot for most goals.

The final award was the MVP—and my name was the one called.

As the crowd cheered, I blinked over and over, stunned as I walked to the podium set up in the middle of the field. Had they made a mistake? Was this really happening? Cameras flashed as the organizers handed me a trophy that I clutched to my chest on the long walk back to my team.

After that, the Bayonets accepted a plaque for their second place finish, and my teammates and I lifted the first place prize—a giant silver cup—high over our heads.

⚽ ⚽ ⚽

In the dressing room, Aron walked over to me. "You deserved that award, Leo. Congrats."

"It could easily have been yours. You played amazing."

He looked off to the side. "Before this tournament, I would have been upset that I didn't win the MVP or the Golden Boot. Now I don't care. My team won! I might not have had the most goals, but I *did* score the most important one, thanks to you." He hesitated. "You know, I appreciate that advice you gave me at Camp Nou. I didn't when you said it, but I do now. I *was* being a selfish ball hog."

"You sure were," Eddy said, slinging an arm around Aron's shoulder.

Aron gave him a playful shove, and the rest of the team joined in, whooping and yelling and wrestling in the dressing room.

"Ah, excuse me," Coach Beppe said, holding up a finger. He was clutching a cell phone in his other hand.

"Did you find a good pasta restaurant?" Patrick asked, causing us all to laugh.

"Not yet," Coach Beppe said solemnly. "But I do have a message from Samantha. Would you like to hear it now, or—" he glared at Patrick—"after dinner?"

"Now, Coach Bep!" John cried, and the rest of us shouted our agreement.

"Ah, *sí*, well, here it is." Coach Beppe cleared his throat. "She says, and I quote: 'I just heard about the win. Congratulations, Knights, I'm so very proud of you. What an incredible run! Oh—and welcome back to the youth Premier League.'"

"The Premier League," I said in a daze, almost forgetting what had been at stake in the tournament. "Wait—the *Premier League!*"

I wasn't sure what was better, winning the Tournament of Champions or securing our return to the English top division next season.

It didn't matter, I thought, as my teammates began to celebrate all over again.

Because we didn't have to choose.

⚽ ⚽ ⚽

In the morning, our last day in Paris and of the entire summer trip, Coach Beppe let us decide what we wanted to do. We voted for three repeats: seeing the Eiffel Tower, boating down the Seine River, and visiting Montmartre for chocolate crepes.

We took the boat ride in the morning this time, seeing the city from a new perspective. The Eiffel Tower was just as impressive as before, and we had fun hanging out in the park surrounding the base of the tower, eating French fries, playing Frisbee, and gazing up at the world-famous monument. After that, we took the metro to Anvers and walked up the long hill to Montmartre. We could have found chocolate crepes anywhere in the city, but the ones in Montmartre had been our favorites, and we liked the cobblestone streets and the views of Paris.

As I took my warm, paper-wrapped crepe from the vendor and enjoyed a bite of gooey chocolate, I grew thoughtful, sad the summer was ending. I realized John and Eddy wouldn't be with us next season. Neither would Caden or Sami. They were all moving up to the U16 division. I would miss my friends like crazy. Even Caden had grown on me. At least I would see them around the academy. And maybe we'd all be on the same team again one day, playing for the Lewisham Knights U16s.

But I knew there was no guarantee that would happen.

This led me to wonder who would replace my friends on our team. Would one of the second-team players step up, or would the coaches recruit someone new? Would Aron stay on the team or return to Switzerland?

Would we finish near the bottom of the league again, or have a title fight on our hands?

After finishing our crepes, we began walking towards Sacré-Coeur, the cathedral at the top of Montmartre. I asked Coach Beppe if I could run ahead. It wasn't that far, and he agreed.

I borrowed a soccer ball from one of the managers—we always had a ball somewhere—and slipped away when my friends weren't looking. There was something I needed to do, and I wanted to do it alone, before the team arrived. Why? I couldn't really say, except that I felt like I had unfinished business, and I needed to complete it without the support of my friends as a crutch.

I hurried down the street and entered the courtyard surrounding Sacré-Coeur. The three domes of the ivory cathedral soared high overhead. I waded through the crush of people and approached the low wall at the top of the steps.

The wall about a foot wide with all the tourists standing in front of it, gazing at the Eiffel Tower in the distance.

So many tourists my stomach felt tight.

This morning, I had worn a baseball cap to help shield my eyes from the sun. I took off the cap, turned it upside down, and set it on the wall.

I almost didn't go through with it. At the beginning of the summer, if I had been by myself, alone in a foreign country, I probably would have snuck away from this wall, too uncomfortable and self-conscious to perform in front of strangers. Why would anyone want to watch Leo K. Doyle, a regular kid from Middleton, Ohio, do anything?

But then, with a deep breath, I hopped on the wall beside the baseball cap and began to juggle. It took me a minute to find my balance, but I was enjoying the routine and began working in some tricks. I did four foot stalls in a row, switching feet each time, completed three around-the-worlds, and got even fancier. More and more people started to watch. Someone began to clap, and before I knew it, a small crowd had gathered.

Now I was nervous. Really, really nervous. All of a sudden, I was embarrassed, too, putting myself out there in front of all these people. I wasn't sure why. I had just played in front of thousands. I knew I was good. But this was different. This was a test of balance and skill, sure, but more than that, I felt as if I was on trial in public. And none of my friends were around to back me up. It was just me, a ball, and some strange need to conquer my fears, ignore what everyone around me was thinking, and do better than I had the last time.

For me, not for them.

I threw in some more around-the-worlds, side stalls, and heel pops. I almost stumbled, causing a few gasps in the crowd, but threw out my arms and regained my balance.

Coins began to drop in the hat. I got fancier and fancier. The crossover Tig had taught me at the London airport, some rabonas in midair, and then some really difficult reverse toe bounces.

Just like last time, a few hecklers moved to the front row,

a group of older teenagers with sneers, tight shirts, and greasy hair. They had probably seen people try to juggle on this wall before and were determined to make me stumble. They probably thought I was lame and skinny and dumb. I grimaced and kept going, faster and faster, more tricks and more tricks and even trying the handstand I had seen that pro guy do the last time I was here—

That one got me. I fell off the wall and landed in the bushes. As I brushed myself off and climbed back over, embarrassed, some of the crowd clapped in appreciation, but the teens in the front row jeered and clutched their bellies as if my fall was the funniest thing they'd ever seen.

I didn't care. I had accomplished my goal.

I had proved to myself I could stand on that wall alone.

Up above, at the edge of the courtyard, I saw my team arriving. They hadn't noticed me yet. I picked up my ball in one arm and my hat in the other. It had more money in it than I had realized. I hesitated, then carried it to a woman begging in front of the cathedral. Just as Coach Beppe had done, I gave her all the money, feeling good about it, then turned around when someone chucked me on the shoulder.

I cringed, thinking those teens in the front row were trying to start something. Instead, I was surprised to see the same short, muscular man we had seen juggling on the wall the last time. He was carrying a boom box on one shoulder and holding a ball in his other hand. I guess he was about to start his show.

He set the boom box down. "Nice job, kid."

"You saw that?"

"Sure did. It was brave. And you've got real talent. But why'd you do it? I saw you give the money away."

"I . . . don't really know. I didn't do so well the last time."

He regarded me with pursed lips. "That's it?"

I looked away. "I guess. Yeah."

"Mm hmm," he said with a knowing tone. "It isn't easy getting on that wall alone."

I faced him again. "Are you a pro? Or were you?"

"Almost. I got injured and had to change careers." He hesitated, then took a leather necklace out from under his shirt. There was a charm on it, a curved and wicked-looking tooth almost two inches long. It wasn't polished white like the shark teeth you see in stores, but had beige and yellow splotches that made it seem genuine.

He lifted the necklace over his head and clutched it in his fist. "I'm from Senegal, you know. When I was about your age, I found this tooth in the hills. It belonged to a young lion."

My eyes widened. "Oh."

"My mother made this necklace for me. She died when I was young, so it became my good luck charm on the field. After my career ended, I wanted to pass it on one day, but I was never sure who to give it to. When I saw you on that wall by yourself . . ." He held it out. "Here. I want you to have it."

I was stunned by the offer. He didn't even know my name was Leo, which means *lion*.

Or that my mom had died when I was young too, and that lions were her favorite animal and that's why she had chosen my name.

"I don't think I should," I said. "That's your good luck charm."

"As I said, it *was*." He thrust it forward again. "Please, take it. Such things should be passed on in life. Maybe you'll get further than I did. Make it to the pros one day."

Touched by the offer, I accepted the gift and rubbed my thumb against the sharp tip of the tooth, captivated by its size.

"Good luck," he said, then carried his boom box to the low wall, turned on the music, and began to juggle far more impressively than I had. As a much bigger crowd gathered, I watched him for a bit, awed and humbled by his talent.

If I'm gonna be a pro one day, I've got a long way to go.

Eventually I turned and saw my team gathered in front of the cathedral. No one had noticed me yet—except Coach Beppe. He was standing on the top step, looking right at me with his arms crossed. How much had he seen, I wondered? Had he watched me juggle or did he just walk up?

Though he was pretty far away, I felt sure I saw him wink in my direction before he turned and walked towards the cathedral, craning his neck so he could see the top of the ivory dome.

I turned back for a glimpse of Paris. The sun had started to set, casting a red glow over the Eiffel Tower. After slipping the leather necklace around my neck and tucking it beneath my shirt, I climbed the steps to rejoin my team, feeling good, thinking about my mom and my future and the challenges next season would bring.

**COMING SUMMER 2024!
THE ACADEMY IV: TITLE FIGHT**

To stay up to date on the Academy Series and other stories by T.Z. Layton, it's best to join his New Release Newsletter:

subscribepage.com/tzlaytonbooks

Acknowledgments

Thanks once again to David Downing for getting the vibe of this story and editing with just the right touch. Meredith Tennant provided expert copyediting, and Jaye Manus polishes every book she works on like a rare diamond. My Dream Team of advance readers— Zara, Ella, John, and Deborah—remained in place and gave so much invaluable support and feedback. I couldn't do it without you (nor would I want to). Tinashe Chidarikire helps ensure my soccer knowledge is always on-point and helps out in a myriad of ways that are hugely appreciated. And I feel so lucky to have the immensely talented Robert Ball working on the cover art.

Finally, I am so appreciative of my young readers who are following along with Leo and his friends on their journey. Your dreams give life to their story.

About the Author

T.Z. Layton is bestselling author Layton Green's pen name for books aimed at younger readers. The author's novels have been nominated for many awards, translated into multiple languages, and optioned for film. The author is also a soccer dad, youth coach, referee, former collegiate player, and lifelong fan of the beautiful game.

Word of mouth is crucial to the success of any author. If you enjoyed Leo's adventures, please consider leaving an honest review on Goodreads, Amazon, Barnes & Noble, or another book site, even if it's only a line or two. (Note: if you're under 13, please ask a parent to help you.)

You can visit T.Z. on Facebook, Goodreads, or at tzlaytonbooks.com for additional information on the author, his works, and more.